PYTHON

FOR

DATA SCIENCE

Comprehensive Guide of Tips and Tricks using Python Data Science Theories

ETHAN WILLIAMS

TABLE OF CONTENTS

Introduction

What Do You Mean by Data Science?

Before we get into the meat of this book, let's just go over what data science is all about. And let's just say, it's not easy to describe given the many connotations and applications regarding data as well as science. First and foremost, data science is a relatively new field that a variety of organizations use to perform data-driven decisions. It is a mix of business, mathematics, and technical knowledge. Data scientists usually wear a ridiculous number of hats to make sense of the data they have and derive whatever value they can out of it. By far, one of the most common programming languages that data scientists use is Python. This is because Python is a language that is simple to understand and use for numerous purposes makes including scripting, application open, and web development among others.

Using Python to perform data science operations is quite powerful since it cleans data at raw levels to develop sophisticated machine learning algorithms that can foresee retail company customer churns. This book covers an assortment of data science concepts in a structured format, along with how they can be applied to data and be able to interpret results with them. Furthermore, the book offers a great foundation for helping future data scientists understand advanced data science topics and how they can be applied in the real world.

Perhaps the best way to describe data science is through Drew Conway's Data Science Venn Diagram that he published on his blog in September 2010. In other words, data science lies at the intersection of:

- Hacking skills

- Substantive expertise

- Math and statistics knowledge

The goal here is to help users develop the hacking skills they required to start doing data science. And for those who are not huge fans of mathematics or statistics which are the backbone of data science, rest assured, we'll be sure to break it to you in a way that won't give you a migraine.

By reading this book, you have a good grasp of how to hack on things with the right tools at your disposal. You'll even get a good understanding of how to approach data problems.

Likewise, you also need to learn mathematics along the way, like understanding statistics, probability, and linear algebra if you're able to have any hope of using data science the right way. This means we'll also be covering mathematical intuition, mathematical axioms, mathematical equations, as well as complex mathematical ideas, which we assure you won't scare you.

Ultimately, our goal is to enable you to have fun with data.

Who Does This Book Benefit?

This book doesn't necessarily teach readers about what Python is or how they can learn to program in general. Rather, it is for those who are already Python developers who already possess some degree of data science knowledge, including assigning variables, defining functions, controlling a program's flow calling object methods and other fundamental skills and now wish to advance to the next level. This book will help users learn how to use Python's stack of data science–libraries of data science that include NumPy, Matplotlib, Pandas and similar tools – to manipulate, store, and gain valuable data insight.

If you're a beginner, worry not as we'll be approaching data science from scratch. What this means is that you'll learn to build tools and implement algorithms by hand so you can understand them better. Throughout the book, you'll learn how to use libraries and then apply the techniques you learn to larger data sets.

Besides Python, other programming languages can be used to learn data science. Most believe that it's the statistical programming language R, whereas others have suggested Scala or Java. But the reason why we went with Python is that it's free, quite simple to code in, and has plenty of data science-related libraries that are very useful.

Python's usefulness comes mainly from the active and enormous environment of third-party packages: Pandas for manipulation of labeled and heterogeneous data, NumPy for homogeneous array-like data manipulation, Matplotlib for publication-quality visualizations, SciPy for recurring scientific computing operations, Scikit-Learn for machine learning, IPython for interactive sharing and execution of code and several other tools that we will cover later on in this book.

Downloading Code Examples

You can download supplemental material such as code examples and figures by visiting https://github.com/jakevdp/PythonDataScienceHandbook. You can use the book to help get the job done. If the book has an example code, it can be utilized the programs you make as well as documentation. There's no reason for you to seek our permission unless you're reproducing a huge part of any code. Like for instance, whenever you write a program that utilizes a plethora of codes within this book, you don't require any permission. However, you do need permission if you're planning to sell or distribute an entire CD-ROM of the examples from our books. Another example of where you don't need permission is when you cite this book to answer a question and when you quote an example code.

Considerations for Installation

There's really nothing complex when you install Python and its various libraries that authorize scientific computing. Here, we have outlined some things you need to take into consideration when you're setting your computer up.

Although there are several ways in which Python can be installed, the best one that we recommend is the distribution of Anaconda, which works the same if you're using either Windows, Mac OS X, or Linux. There are two sides to the Anaconda distribution:

- **Anaconda:** which includes both Python and a command-line tool known as *conda,* as well as a bundle of another suite of preinstalled packages designed for scientific computing. Because of its enormous size, the installation could take up an enormous amount of gigabyte disk space.

- **Miniconda:** will give you the Python interpreter along with conda. It functions as a cross-platform package manager that is designed for Python packages, which is in the same manner as the yum or apt tools that will be familiar to Linux users.

You'll also find that any package included with the Anaconda distribution can be installed at the top of Miniconda manually. Therefore, we recommend giving Miniconda a go first.

The first thing you need to do is download and then have the Miniconda package installed (choose a Python 3 version) and then have the same core packages installed that are used in the following book:

[~]$ conda install numpy pandas scikit-learn matplotlib seaborn ipython-notebook

The installation process is a breeze in which you only need to type

conda installpackagename.

Chapter One

Introducing NumPy

Numerical Python, or NumPy for short, is the standard package for data analysis as well as high-performance scientific computing. NumPy serves as the foundation which all of the complex tools mentioned in this book have been built upon. Some of the things that NumPy offers include:

- Standard mathematical functions for quick data array operations without writing loops.

- ndarray, a compact and fast multidimensional array that offers sophisticated broadcasting functionalities and vectorized arithmetic operations.

- Fourier transform functionalities, random number generation, and linear algebra.

- Tools for working with memory-mapped files reading and writing array data onto discs.

- Tools for integrating code written in Fortran, C, and C++.

The last bullet point is very crucial as NumPy offers a C API that is easy to use and makes data transfer to low-level language external libraries easier as well as external libraries to have data returned as NumPy arrays to Python. This is what makes Python a viable choice for grouping legacy C/C++/Fortran code bases and then giving them an interface that is easy to use and dynamic.

Although there aren't much high-level data analytics capabilities that can be found with NumPy on its own, programmers can efficiently use tools like pandas more effectively by developing an understanding of NumPy array and array-focused computing.

NumPy arrays have a vast number of differences from that of standard Python sequences, including:

- NumPy array elements have to be the same data type, and the memory needs to be of the same size. The only difference is that one can have object arrays that can then allow arrays that are of varying sized elements.

- Unlike Python lists, NumPy arrays are created at a fixed size. What this means is that if a ndarray's size changes, a new array will be created, and the original will be deleted.

- A growing number of mathematical and scientific packages based on Python use NumPy arrays; even though they usually support input from Python sequence, they were able to convert that input to NumPy arrays before processing, and NumPy arrays are often outputted. To be more specific, if one is to use most of today's mathematical/scientific Python-based software, simply knowing the building sequin types of Python is not enough – they also need to understand the proper use of NumPy arrays.

- NumPy arrays perform complex mathematical and large data type operations. Though using Python's built-in sequences, these operations can be performed more efficiently and with less complex coding involved.

The NumPy ndarray

The ndarray or N-dimensional array object is one of the most important features of NumPy. It is a flexible and fast container capable of storing large Python data sets. Arrays allow you to perform mathematical operations on whole blocks of data using syntax identical to operations between scalar elements:

In [8]: data

Out[8]:

array([[0.9526, -0.246 , -0.8856],

[0.5639, 0.2379, 0.9104]])

In [9]: data * 10 In [10]: data + data

Out[9]: Out[10]:

array([[9.5256, -2.4601, -8.8565], array([[1.9051, -0.492 , -1.7713],

[5.6385, 2.3794, 9.104]]) [1.1277, 0.4759, 1.8208]])

An ndarray is a standard multidimensional container for homogenous data; in other words, every element has to be the exact type. Each array comes with a shape, a tuple that indicates every dimension's size, and an object known as dtype, that describes the array's datatype:

In [11]: data.shape

Out[11]: (2, 3)

In [12]: data.dtype

Out[12]: dtype('float64')

Over here, you will learn the fundamentals of how to use NumPy arrays, which should be just enough to get you to understand the rest of the book. Of course, it's not really necessary for you to have an incredible understanding of NumPy for numerous data analytical operations, you should have a good understanding of array-focused programming as well as thinking to become a Python data scientist.

How to Create ndarrays

The best way to create an array is with the 'array' function. Any sequence-like object (like other arrays) can be used here, in which a new NumPy array that contains the passed data is produced. A list, for example, is an ideal conversion candidate:

In [13]: data1 = [6, 7.5, 8, 0, 1]

In [14]: arr1 = np.array(data1)

In [15]: arr1

Out[15]: array([6. , 7.5, 8. , 0. , 1.])

Nested sequences, such as a list of equal-length lists, can be converted into a multidimensional array:

In [16]: data2 = [[1, 2, 3, 4], [5, 6, 7, 8]]

In [17]: arr2 = np.array(data2)

In [18]: arr2

Out[18]:

array([[1, 2, 3, 4],

[5, 6, 7, 8]])

In [19]: arr2.ndim

Out[19]: 2

In [20]: arr2.shape

Out[20]: (2, 4)

Unless specified explicitly, 'np.array' will attempt to infer a good data type for the array that it generates. This datatype gets stored in special dtype object. For instance, for the first two examples, we have:

In [21]: arr1.dtype

Out[21]: dtype('float64')

In [22]: arr2.dtype

Out[22]: dtype('int64')

Besides np.array, several more functions for creating new arrays exist. For example, ones and zeros create arrays of 1's and 0's, respectively, with a given shape or length. Without initializing its values to any one value, 'empty' will create an array. If you want to use these methods to create a higher dimensional array, has a tuple for the shape:

In [23]: np.zeros(10)

Out[23]: array([0., 0., 0., 0., 0., 0., 0., 0., 0., 0.])

In [24]: np.zeros((3, 6))

Out[24]:

array([[0., 0., 0., 0., 0., 0.],

 [0., 0., 0., 0., 0., 0.],

 [0., 0., 0., 0., 0., 0.]])

In [25]: np.empty((2, 3, 2))

Out[25]:

array([[[4.94065646e-324, 4.94065646e-324],

[3.87491056e-297, 2.46845796e-130],

[4.94065646e-324, 4.94065646e-324]],

[[1.90723115e+083, 5.73293533e-053],

[-2.33568637e+124, -6.70608105e-012],

[4.42786966e+160, 1.27100354e+025]]])

'arrange' is the built-in Python 'range' function's array-valued version:

In [26]: np.arange(15)

Out[26]: array([0, 1, 2, 3, 4, 5, 6, 7, 8, 9, 10, 11, 12, 13, 14])

ndarrays Datatypes

The dtype or data type, is a special object that consists of the information that the ndarray requires to interpret a piece of memory as a particular type of data:

In [27]: arr1 = np.array([1, 2, 3], dtype=np.float64)

In [28]: arr2 = np.array([1, 2, 3], dtype=np.int32)

In [29]: arr1.dtype In [30]: arr2.dtype

Out[29]: dtype('float64') Out[30]: dtype('int32')

np.array will infer a good data type for the array that it will create unless explicitly specified. The datatype will be stored in a special dtype object; for instance, in the two examples shared above:

In [21]: arr1.dtype

Out[21]: dtype('float64')

In [22]: arr2.dtype

Out[22]: dtype('int64')

Array Creation Functions

Function	Description
array	Input data converted into a ndarray by either explicitly specifying a dtype or inferring a dtype. Input data is copied by default
arange	similar to a built-in range, but instead of returning as a list, the returns as an ndarray.
asarray	input data converted to ndarray, but should not be copied if the input is already a ndarray
zeros, zeros_like	Produces an array of 0's is given shape, and dtype.zeros_like takes another array and produces a zeros array of the same shape and dtype.
once, ones_like	Like zeros and zeros_like, except produce arrays of 1's instead

eye, identity	creates a square NxN identity matrix
empty, empty_like	new arrays are created by allocating new memory but don't populate with values such as ones and zeros.

The Fundamentals of NumPy Arrays

Python data manipulation is almost interchangeable with NumPy array manipulation: brand-new tools such as pandas have even been built around this array. In this section, we will show you several ways of accessing data and sub-arrays using NumPy array manipulation, and how to reshape, split, and then join arrays. Even though the kinds of operations displayed here might be somewhat dry and unimportant, they are highly essential like many of the other examples that have been used in this book.

We'll be covering the following basic array manipulation categories including:

- **Indexing of arrays**

How to get and set individual array element values

- **Array attributes**

How to determine the shape, size, consumption of memory, and array data types.

- **Reshaping arrays**

How to change the shape of an array

- **Slicing arrays**

How to get and set smaller sub-arrays in a larger array.

- **Join and split arrays**

How to combine several arrays as one and then split one into several others

Attributes of NumPy Array

Let's first look at some array attributes. Let's start by talking about three arrays: 1D, 2D, and 3D array. Using the random number generator of NumPy, a set value will be seeded so that every time the code runs, the same arrays are produced all the time.

In[1]: import numpy as np

np.random.seed(0) # seed for reproducibility

x1 = np.random.randint(10, size=6) # One-dimensional array

x2 = np.random.randint(10, size=(3, 4)) # Two-dimensional array

x3 = np.random.randint(10, size=(3, 4, 5)) # Three-dimensional array

Every array consists of attributes such as shape (size of every dimension), size (total array size), and ndim (number of dimensions):

In[2]: print("x3 ndim: ", x3.ndim)

print("x3 shape:", x3.shape)

print("x3 size: ", x3.size)

x3 ndim: 3

x3 shape: (3, 4, 5)

x3 size: 60

dtype, the array's data type is another excellent attribute:

In[3]: print("dtype:", x3.dtype)

dtype: int64

Another attribute is the 'itemsize,' in which the size of every array element is listed, and nbytes, where the array's total size is listed:

In[4]: print("itemsize:", x3.itemsize, "bytes")

 print("nbytes:", x3.nbytes, "bytes")

itemsize: 8 bytes

nbytes: 480 bytes

It may be assumed that 'nbytes' equals 'itemsize' times 'size.'

Array Indexing

If you know about the standard list indexing of Python, then NumPy indexing will feel similar. The ith value may be accessed in a one-dimensional array when the required index of square brackets have been specified, just like Python lists:

In[5]: x1

Out[5]: array([5, 0, 3, 3, 7, 9])

In[6]: x1[0]

Out[6]: 5

In[7]: x1[4]

Out[7]: 7

For an index from the array's end, negative indices should be used:

In[8]: x1[-1]

Out[8]: 9

In[9]: x1[-2]

Out[9]: 7

We can access items in a multidimensional array using a tuple of indices, separated by commas:

In[10]: x2

Out[10]: array([[3, 5, 2, 4],

[7, 6, 8, 8],

[1, 6, 7, 7]])

In[11]: x2[0, 0]

Out[11]: 3

In[12]: x2[2, 0]

Out[12]: 1

In[13]: x2[2, -1]

Out[13]: 7

You can use any of these index notations to modify values:

In[14]: x2[0, 0] = 12

x2

Out[14]: array([[12, 5, 2, 4],

[7, 6, 8, 8],

[1, 6, 7, 7]])

It's worth noting that NumPy arrays, unlike Python lists, are fixed in type. If, for instance, a floating-point value has been inserted into an array of integers, the value is truncated silently. Be sure to be very wary of behavior like this.

In[15]: x1[0] = 3.14159 # this will be truncated!

x1

Out[15]: array([3, 0, 3, 3, 7, 9])

Slicing of Arrays

Like how they can be used to access separate array elements, square brackets may also use the slice notation – indicated by the character colon (:) to access subarrays. Like the basic Python list, an array slice, x, can be accessed using the NumPy slicing syntax, which goes like:

x[start:stop:step]

Should any of the values be unspecified, they will default to step=1, stop=size of dimension, and start=0. Here's how some arrays can be accessed in a single dimension as well as several dimensions:

One-Dimensional Subarrays

In[16]: x = np.arange(10)

x

Out[16]: array([0, 1, 2, 3, 4, 5, 6, 7, 8, 9])

In[17]: x[:5] # first five elements

Out[17]: array([0, 1, 2, 3, 4])

In[18]: x[5:] # elements after index 5

Out[18]: array([5, 6, 7, 8, 9])

In[19]: x[4:7] # middle subarray

Out[19]: array([4, 5, 6])

In[20]: x[::2] # every other element

Out[20]: array([0, 2, 4, 6, 8])

In[21]: x[1::2] # every other element, starting at index 1

Out[21]: array([1, 3, 5, 7, 9])

A confusing matter is when we have a negative step value. Over here, the stop and start defaults have been swapped. This offers an easy way to get an array reversed:

In[22]: x[::-1] # all elements, reversed

Out[22]: array([9, 8, 7, 6, 5, 4, 3, 2, 1, 0])

In[23]: x[5::-2] # reversed every other from index 5

Out[23]: array([5, 3, 1])

Multidimensional Subarrays

Slices for multidimensional sub-arrays work the same way; several slices that are divided by commas. For instance:

In[24]: x2

Out[24]: array([[12, 5, 2, 4],

[7, 6, 8, 8],

[1, 6, 7, 7]])

In[25]: x2[:2, :3] # two rows, three columns

Out[25]: array([[12, 5, 2],

[7, 6, 8]])

In[26]: x2[:3, ::2] # all rows, every other column

Out[26]: array([[12, 2],

[7, 8],

[1, 7]])

Lastly, dimensions for every separate can be reversed as well:

In[27]: x2[::-1, ::-1]

Out[27]: array([[7, 7, 6, 1],

[8, 8, 6, 7],

[4, 2, 5, 12]])

How to Access Array Columns and Rows

One of the most important routines is being able to access single array columns or rows. We can do this with a combination of slicing and indexing, with an empty sliced that's been marked with one (:):

In[28]: print(x2[:, 0]) # first column of x2

[12 7 1]

In[29]: print(x2[0, :]) # first row of x2

[12 5 2 4]

When it comes to row access, shorter syntax can be used in place of the empty slice:

In[30]: print(x2[0]) # equivalent to x2[0, :]

[12 5 2 4]

How to Create Array Copies

Sometimes, copying the data explicitly within an array or subarray is useful despite the great array view features. You can do this using the copy () method:

In[35]: x2_sub_copy = x2[:2, :2].copy()

print(x2_sub_copy)

[[99 5]

 [7 6]]

The original array will not be touched even if we modify the subarray:

In[36]: x2_sub_copy[0, 0] = 42

print(x2_sub_copy)

[[42 5]

 [7 6]]

In[37]: print(x2)

[[99 5 2 4]

 [7 6 8 8]

 [1 6 7 7]]

No-Copy Views Subarrays

The thing with array slices is the array data's *views* are returned
instead of *copies*. This is where array slicing in NumPy is different
from Python slicing: slices will become copies in lists. Let's look back
at a 2D array from earlier:

In[31]: print(x2)

[[12 5 2 4]

 [7 6 8 8]

 [1 6 7 7]]

Now let's have a 2x2 separate extracted from it:

In[32]: x2_sub = x2[:2, :2]

print(x2_sub)

[[12 5]

[7 6]]

When the subarray has been modified, the original array will have changed as the following indicates:

In[33]: x2_sub[0, 0] = 99

print(x2_sub)

[[99 5]

 [7 6]]

In[34]: print(x2)

[[99 5 2 4]

 [7 6 8 8]

 [1 6 7 7]]

This is default behavior and is quite powerful because when it allows us to work with larger data sets, these data sets can be processed and accessed without copying the underlying data buffer.

Operations Between Scalars and Arrays

Arrays are essential because you can express batch operations on data without the need of any 'for' loops. This is known as vectorization. Arithmetic operations that are carried out between equal-size arrays have the same operations applied elementwise:

In [45]: arr = np.array([[1., 2., 3.], [4., 5., 6.]])

In [46]: arr

Out[46]:

array([[1., 2., 3.],

[4., 5., 6.]])

In [47]: arr * arr   In [48]: arr - arr

Out[47]: Out[48]:

array([[1., 4., 9.], array([[0., 0., 0.],

[16., 25., 36.]]) [0., 0., 0.]])

Arithmetic operations with scalars propagate value to every element:

In [49]: 1 / arr   In [50]: arr ** 0.5

Out[49]: Out[50]:

array([[1. , 0.5 , 0.3333], array([[1. , 1.4142, 1.7321],

[0.25 , 0.2 , 0.1667]]) [2. , 2.2361, 2.4495]])

Operations carried out between arrays of varying sizes are known as broadcasting. Fortunately, you don't need to have a broad understanding of broadcasting for this book.

Boolean Indexing

Let's take an example will be have some array data as well as an array consisting of names duplicates. For 'numpy.random' we're going to use the 'randn' function in 'numpy.random' to generate some random data that's normally distributed:

In [83]: names = np.array(['Bob', 'Joe', 'Will', 'Bob', 'Will', 'Joe', 'Joe'])

In [84]: data = randn(7, 4)

In [85]: names

Out[85]:

array(['Bob', 'Joe', 'Will', 'Bob', 'Will', 'Joe', 'Joe'],

 dtype='|S4')

In [86]: data

Out[86]:

array([[-0.048 , 0.5433, -0.2349, 1.2792],

 [-0.268 , 0.5465, 0.0939, -2.0445],

 [-0.047 , -2.026 , 0.7719, 0.3103],

 [2.1452, 0.8799, -0.0523, 0.0672],

 [-1.0023, -0.1698, 1.1503, 1.7289],

 [0.1913, 0.4544, 0.4519, 0.5535],

 [0.5994, 0.8174, -0.9297, -1.2564]])

Let's assume that each name corresponds to a row from the 'data' array. We'll pick every row that corresponds with the name 'Bob.' Similar to recommended functions, comparisons with arrays are also vectorized. Hence, comparing 'names' with the string "Bob' yields a Boolean array:

In [87]: names == 'Bob'

Out[87]: array([True, False, False, True, False, False, False],
dtype=bool)

You can pass this array after it has been indexed:

In [88]: data[names == 'Bob']

Out[88]:

array([[-0.048 , 0.5433, -0.2349, 1.2792],

[2.1452, 0.8799, -0.0523, 0.0672]])

The axis that is being indexed needs to be of the same length as the Boolean array. Boolean arrays can be mixed and matched with integers or slices:

In [89]: data[names == 'Bob', 2:]

Out[89]:

array([[-0.2349, 1.2792],

[-0.0523, 0.0672]])

In [90]: data[names == 'Bob', 3]

Out[90]: array([1.2792, 0.0672])

If you want to pick anything except 'Bob', you can use either '!=' Or negate the condition with '-':

In [91]: names != 'Bob'

Out[91]: array([False, True, True, False, True, True, True],
dtype=bool)

In [92]: data[-(names == 'Bob')]

Out[92]:

array([[-0.268 , 0.5465, 0.0939, -2.0445],

[-0.047 , -2.026 , 0.7719, 0.3103],

[-1.0023, -0.1698, 1.1503, 1.7289],

[0.1913, 0.4544, 0.4519, 0.5535],

[0.5994, 0.8174, -0.9297, -1.2564]])

If you're going to combine several Boolean conditions by choosing two of the three names, use Boolean arithmetic operators '| (or)' and '& (and)':

In [93]: mask = (names == 'Bob') | (names == 'Will')

In [94]: mask

Out[94]: array([True, False, True, True, True, False, False], dtype=bool)

In [95]: data[mask]

Out[95]:

array([[-0.048 , 0.5433, -0.2349, 1.2792],

[-0.047 , -2.026 , 0.7719, 0.3103],

[2.1452, 0.8799, -0.0523, 0.0672],

[-1.0023, -0.1698, 1.1503, 1.7289]])

If you choose data from a Boolean indexing array, a copy of the data will always be created, even if the returned array has not been changed.

It's common sense as to how values with Boolean array are set. If you want to set every negative value and data to zero, all you need to do is:

In [96]: data[data < 0] = 0

In [97]: data

Out[97]:

array([[0. , 0.5433, 0. , 1.2792],

[0. , 0.5465, 0.0939, 0.],

[0. , 0. , 0.7719, 0.3103],

[2.1452, 0.8799, 0. , 0.0672],

[0. , 0. , 1.1503, 1.7289],

[0.1913, 0.4544, 0.4519, 0.5535],

[0.5994, 0.8174, 0. , 0.]])

It's also very easy to set entire columns and rows with a 1D Boolean array:

In [98]: data[names != 'Joe'] = 7

In [99]: data

Out[99]:

array([[7. , 7. , 7. , 7.],

[0. , 0.5465, 0.0939, 0.],

[7. , 7. , 7. , 7.],

[7. , 7. , 7. , 7.],

[7. , 7. , 7. , 7.],

[0.1913, 0.4544, 0.4519, 0.5535],

[0.5994, 0.8174, 0. , 0.]])

Fancy Indexing

Here, we will take a look at fancy indexing, which is another form of array indexing. This is like the regular indexing that we've just seen, but use single scalars instead of an array of indices. With this, complex subsets of the values of an array can be accessed and modified quickly.

Looking at the Fancy Indexing

This type of indexing is pretty much a simple concept: it is when an array of indices are passed in order to access numerous array elements at the same time. Let's look at the given array as an example:

```
In[1]: import numpy as np

rand = np.random.RandomState(42)

x = rand.randint(100, size=10)

print(x)

[51 92 14 71 60 20 82 86 74 74]
```

If you want to access three different elements, we could do something like this:

In[2]: [x[3], x[7], x[2]]

Out[2]: [71, 86, 14]

on the other hand, we can acquire the same result by passing a single list or an array of indices:

In[3]: ind = [3, 7, 4]

x[ind]

Out[3]: array([71, 86, 60])

fancy indexing is when the ship we see in the result reflects the shape we see in the *index arrays* instead of the array's shape being indexed:

In[4]: ind = np.array([[3, 7],

[4, 5]])

x[ind]

Out[4]: array([[71, 86],

[60, 20]])

Similar to basic indexing, the first index represents the row and the 2nd one represents the column:

In[6]: row = np.array([0, 1, 2])

col = np.array([2, 1, 3])

X[row, col]

Out[6]: array([2, 5, 11])

You'll see how the first value is shown in the result is X[0, 2], X[1, 1] in the second, and X[2, 3] the third. So if we were to, let's say, combine a row vector and a column vector inside the indices, we would get a two-dimensional result:

In[7]: X[row[:, np.newaxis], col]

Out[7]: array([[2, 1, 3],

[6, 5, 7],

[10, 9, 11]])

Over here, just as we've seen in broadcasting of arithmetic operations, every row has been matched with every column vector. For instance:

In[8]: row[:, np.newaxis] * col

Out[8]: array([[0, 0, 0],

[2, 1, 3],

[4, 2, 6]])

It should always be considered that the return value reflects the indices' broadcasted shape when it comes to fancy indexing, instead of the array's shape being indexed.

How to Use Fancy Indexing to Modify Values

Like how fancy indexing can access parts of an array, it can even modify parts of an array as well. Let's say, we have an array of indices and that we want to set the corresponding items in an array to some value:

In[18]: x = np.arange(10)

29

```
i = np.array([2, 1, 8, 4])

x[i] = 99

print(x)

[ 0 99 99 3 99 5 6 7 99 9]
```

You can use any assignment-type operator for this, such as:

```
In[19]: x[i] -= 10

print(x)

[ 0 89 89 3 89 5 6 7 89 9]
```

There is, however, the possibility of potentially unexpected results that are caused by repeated and dices with these types of operations. for example:

```
In[20]: x = np.zeros(10)

x[[0, 0]] = [4, 6]

print(x)

[ 6. 0. 0. 0. 0. 0. 0. 0. 0. 0.]
```

Notice how the 4 is gone. The operation was to first have $x[0] = 4$ assigned, then $x[0] = 6$. but the results revealed that $x[0]$ has the value 6.

That is a fair understanding, but the following operation should be considered:

```
In[21]: i = [2, 3, 3, 4, 4, 4]
```

x[i] += 1

x

Out[21]: array([6., 0., 1., 1., 1., 0., 0., 0., 0., 0.])

One should expect x[3] to contain the value of 2, and X [4] should contain the value of 3, considering this is the number of times every index has been repeated. So why isn't this the case? This is because conceptually, x[i] += 1 is supposed to be a shortcut of x[i] = x[i] + 1. x[i] + 1 will be evaluated and then the result will then be assigned to indices in x. Because of this, instead of the augmentation happening several times, the assignment brings about non-intuitive results.

So, if you wanted the behavior where the operation is repeated, you must use the at() method of ufuncs and do the following:

In[22]: x = np.zeros(10)

np.add.at(x, i, 1)

print(x)

[0. 0. 1. 2. 3. 0. 0. 0. 0. 0.]

The at() method makes the given operator's in-place application as specified indices (here, i) with the specified value (here, 1). Another similar method is the reducact() method of ufuncs.

Example: Binning Data

You can efficiently bin data so that a histogram can be created by hand. for instance, let's say that we have over 1000 values and would like to find where they fall in an array of bins quickly. We can use ufunc.at to compute it like this:

In[23]: np.random.seed(42)

```
x = np.random.randn(100)

# compute a histogram by hand

bins = np.linspace(-5, 5, 20)

counts = np.zeros_like(bins)

# find the appropriate bin for each x

i = np.searchsorted(bins, x)

# add 1 to each of these bins

np.add.at(counts, i, 1)
```

Now the count reflects the amount of points in each bin– otherwise known as a histogram.

In[24]: # plot the results

plt.plot(bins, counts, linestyle='steps');

Of course, you don't really have to do this every time you want a histogram plotted. That's exactly why you need Matplotlib which offers the plt.hist() routine that can do the same thing in only a single line:

plt.hist(x, bins, histtype='step');

This function creates a similar plot to the one that's seen here. In order to compute binning, The np.histogram function is used by Matplotlib, which does remarkably identical computation like the one we've seen before. Let's first compare the two right here:

In[25]: print("NumPy routine:")

```
%timeit counts, edges = np.histogram(x, bins)

print("Custom routine:")

%timeit np.add.at(counts, np.searchsorted(bins, x), 1)
```

NumPy routine:

10000 loops, best of 3: 97.6 μs per loop

Custom routine:

10000 loops, best of 3: 19.5 μs per loop

You will see that the one line algorithm we used here is 20 times faster than NumPy's optimized algorithm. Why is this so? If you look into the np.histogram source code, you'll notice that it's a little more involved then the basic search-and-count that we've already done; the reason why this is the case is that there's more flexibility in NumPy's algorithm, and it's obviously built to offer better performance when data point numbers get large:

```
In[26]: x = np.random.randn(1000000)

print("NumPy routine:")

%timeit counts, edges = np.histogram(x, bins)

print("Custom routine:")

%timeit np.add.at(counts, np.searchsorted(bins, x), 1)
```

NumPy routine:

10 loops, best of 3: 68.7 ms per loop

Custom routine:

10 loops, best of 3: 135 ms per loop

Based on this comparison, algorithmic efficiency is never quite simple. It's not always a good idea to have an algorithmic efficient for large data sets apply for small data sets or vice versa. But the benefit of being able to code the algorithm on your own is that you can use them as building blocks to make interesting custom behaviors. When using Python in data-intensive applications, it is essential to learn about general convenience routines such as np.histogram whenever their appropriate, but also learn how to utilize lower-level functionality when you require more pointed behavior.

Combined Indexing

Fancy indexing can also be combined with other indexing schemes that we've seen for more powerful operations:

In[9]: print(X)

[[0 1 2 3]

 [4 5 6 7]

 [8 9 10 11]]

Fancy and simple indices can be combined to give us:

In[10]: X[2, [2, 0, 1]]

Out[10]: array([10, 8, 9])

Fancy indexing can also be combined with slicing:

In[11]: X[1:, [2, 0, 1]]

Out[11]: array([[6, 4, 5],

[10, 8, 9]])

Furthermore, fancy indexing can be combined with masking like:

In[12]: mask = np.array([1, 0, 1, 0], dtype=bool)

X[row[:, np.newaxis], mask]

Out[12]: array([[0, 2],

[4, 6],

[8, 10]])

Each of these indexing options combined results in a set of very flexible operations that allow us to access and modify array values.

Example: Choosing Random Points

Fancy indexing can be commonly used to select subsets of roles from a matrix. for instance, may have a matrix of N by D that represents N points in D dimensions, like the points below that were drawn from a two-dimensional normal distribution:

In[13]: mean = [0, 0]

cov = [[1, 2],

[2, 5]]

X = rand.multivariate_normal(mean, cov, 100)

X.shape

Out[13]: (100, 2)

The points can be visualized as a scatterplot as shown below:

```
In[14]: %matplotlib inline

import matplotlib.pyplot as plt

import seaborn; seaborn.set() # for plot styling

plt.scatter(X[:, 0], X[:, 1]);
```

Let's try using fancy indexing to pick 20 random points. first let's choose 20 random indices without any repeats, and then use them to choose a portion of the original array:

```
In[15]: indices = np.random.choice(X.shape[0], 20,
replace=False)

indices

Out[15]: array([93, 45, 73, 81, 50, 10, 98, 94, 4, 64, 65, 89,
47, 84, 82,

80, 25, 90, 63, 20])

In[16]: selection = X[indices] # fancy indexing here

selection.shape

Out[16]: (20, 2)
```

Now let's have a look at the points that were chosen, and over-plot large circles at the location of the chosen points:

```
In[17]: plt.scatter(X[:, 0], X[:, 1], alpha=0.3)

plt.scatter(selection[:, 0], selection[:, 1],

facecolor='none', s=200);
```

This strategy is used at times to quickly partition data sets, as is required in test/train splitting for validating statistical models, and to answer statistical questions in sampling approaches.

Transposing Arrays and Swapping Access

Transposing is a special type of reshaping which returns a view in an identical manner on the underlying data without having to copy anything. A race can use the transpose method as well as the special 'T' attribute:

In [110]: arr = np.arange(15).reshape((3, 5))

In [111]: arr In [112]: arr.T

Out[111]: Out[112]:

array([[0, 1, 2, 3, 4], array([[0, 5, 10],

 [5, 6, 7, 8, 9], [1, 6, 11],

 [10, 11, 12, 13, 14]]) [2, 7, 12],

 [3, 8, 13],

 [4, 9, 14]])

This will be done quite often when it comes to matrix computations, like when you're using np.dot to compute the inner matrix product XTX:

In [113]: arr = np.random.randn(6, 3)

In [114]: np.dot(arr.T, arr)

Out[114]:

array([[2.584 , 1.8753, 0.8888],

[1.8753, 6.6636, 0.3884],

[0.8888, 0.3884, 3.9781]])

For higher dimensional arrays, a tuple of access numbers will be accepted by transpose to permit the axes:

In [115]: arr = np.arange(16).reshape((2, 2, 4))

In [116]: arr

Out[116]:

array([[[0, 1, 2, 3],

[4, 5, 6, 7]],

[[8, 9, 10, 11],

[12, 13, 14, 15]]])

In [117]: arr.transpose((1, 0, 2))

Out[117]:

array([[[0, 1, 2, 3],

[8, 9, 10, 11]],

[[4, 5, 6, 7],

[12, 13, 14, 15]]])

Basic transposing with '.T' is a special swapping axes case. ndarray has the swapaxes method in which a pair of axis numbers are taken:

In [118]: arr In [119]: arr.swapaxes(1, 2)

Out[118]: Out[119]:

array([[[0, 1, 2, 3], array([[[0, 4],

[4, 5, 6, 7]], [1, 5],

[2, 6],

[[8, 9, 10, 11], [3, 7]],

[12, 13, 14, 15]]])

[[8, 12],

[9, 13],

[10, 14],

[11, 15]]])

swapaxes likewise, returns a view on the data without having to copy anything.

Chapter Two

Manipulating Data with Pandas

In the last chapter, we went into detail about NumPy as well as its ndarray object, offering efficient storage as well as manipulation of dense type Python arrays. We'll look at the great details at the panda's library data structures. Pandas is a relatively newer package that was built on top of NumPy and offered an efficient DataFrame implementation. Basically, DataFrames are multidimensional arrays with attached column and row labels, and sometimes with heterogeneous types and/or missing data. Other than providing convenient label data storage interface, pandas incorporates several powerful data operations identical to users of both database spreadsheets and frameworks programs.

In this chapter will be focusing on the mechanics of how to use DataFrame, Series, as well as other related structures effectively. Using examples taken from real data sets whenever there are appropriate, but they won't necessarily be the focus of our studies going forward.

How to Install and Use Pandas

To have pandas installed on your system, it is important to have NumPy installed first. And if you want to build a library from source, you need to have the proper tools required to compile the C and Cython sources on which pandas has been built. You can use the pandas documentation here for proper installation advice.

Once pandas has been installed, all you need to do is imported and inspect which version has been installed by doing the following:

In[1]: import pandas

pandas.__version__

Out[1]: '0.18.1'

Like how we usually import NumPy using the alias np, we can also import pandas using the alias pd:

In[2]: import pandas as pd

Introducing Pandas Data Structures

To start using pandas, you'll need to get around using it's to work course data structures: *DataFrame* and *Series*. Although these are not a one-size-fits-all solution for each and every problem, they do offer an easy-to-use, solid foundation for many applications.

DataFrame

DataFrames represent a spreadsheet, tabular-like data structure that contains a collection of columns in an orderly fashion, each that can be of a different value type (strained, Boolean, numeric, etc.). DataFrames have a column and row index; it can be assumed as a dict of Series (one that shares the same index). When compared to other types of similar structures that you might have used previously (such as R's data.frame), column-and row-oriented DataFrame operations are roughly treated symmetrically. From within, the data is stored as one or two-dimensional blocks instead of the list, dict, or any other group of one-dimensional arrays. The precise details of the internals of DataFrame is something that we will not cover in this book.

one of the most common out of several other ways to construct a DataFrame is from a dict of NumPy arrays or equal-lengthed lists:

```
data = {'state': ['Ohio', 'Ohio', 'Ohio', 'Nevada', 'Nevada'],

'year': [2000, 2001, 2002, 2001, 2002],

'pop': [1.5, 1.7, 3.6, 2.4, 2.9]}

frame = DataFrame(data)
```

The DataFrame, as a result, will automatically have it index assigned with Series, and the columns will be placed in an organized order:

```
In [38]: frame

Out[38]:

  pop state year

0 1.5 Ohio 2000

1 1.7 Ohio 2001

2 3.6 Ohio 2002

3 2.4 Nevada 2001

4 2.9 Nevada 2002
```

When specifying a sequence of columns, the columns in the DataFrame just is how you pass it:

```
In [39]: DataFrame(data, columns=['year', 'state', 'pop'])

Out[39]:

  year state pop

0 2000 Ohio 1.5
```

1 2001 Ohio 1.7

2 2002 Ohio 3.6

3 2001 Nevada 2.4

4 2002 Nevada 2.9

Just like with Serious, if a column not stored in data has been passed, it will appear with NA values and the result:

In [40]: frame2 = DataFrame(data, columns=['year', 'state', 'pop', 'debt'],

.....: index=['one', 'two', 'three', 'four', 'five'])

In [41]: frame2

Out[41]:

 year state pop debt

one 2000 Ohio 1.5 NaN

two 2001 Ohio 1.7 NaN

three 2002 Ohio 3.6 NaN

four 2001 Nevada 2.4 NaN

five 2002 Nevada 2.9 NaN

In [42]: frame2.columns

Out[42]: Index([year, state, pop, debt], dtype=object)

A DataFrame column can be retrieved as a Series with either a dict-like attribute or by notation:

In [43]: frame2['state'] In [44]: frame2.year

Out[43]: Out[44]:

one Ohio one 2000

two Ohio two 2001

three Ohio three 2002

four Nevada four 2001

five Nevada five 2002

Name: state Name: year

Looking carefully, you will see that the returned Series' index is the same as the DataFrame, with their name attribute being set appropriately.

You can also retrieve a row by name or position using a few methods including the ix indexing field:

In [45]: frame2.ix['three']

Out[45]:

year 2002

state Ohio

pop 3.6

debt NaN

Name: three

You can modify the columns by assignment. For instance, the empty 'debt' column can either be assigned a scalar value or a set of values:

In [46]: frame2['debt'] = 16.5

In [47]: frame2

Out[47]:

 year state pop debt

one 2000 Ohio 1.5 16.5

two 2001 Ohio 1.7 16.5

three 2002 Ohio 3.6 16.5

four 2001 Nevada 2.4 16.5

five 2002 Nevada 2.9 16.5

In [48]: frame2['debt'] = np.arange(5.)

In [49]: frame2

Out[49]:

 year state pop debt

one 2000 Ohio 1.5 0

two 2001 Ohio 1.7 1

three 2002 Ohio 3.6 2

four 2001 Nevada 2.4 3

five 2002 Nevada 2.9 4

When arrays or lists have been assigned to a column, the length of the value has to match the DataFrame's length. If you're assigning a Series, it will conform precisely to the index of the DataFrame, or missing values will be inserted in any hole:

In [50]: val = Series([-1.2, -1.5, -1.7], index=['two', 'four', 'five'])

In [51]: frame2['debt'] = val

In [52]: frame2

Out[52]:

 year state pop debt

one 2000 Ohio 1.5 NaN

two 2001 Ohio 1.7 -1.2

three 2002 Ohio 3.6 NaN

four 2001 Nevada 2.4 -1.5

five 2002 Nevada 2.9 -1.7

When a column that doesn't exist has been assigned, a new column will be created. The del keyword will delete columns as with a dict:

In [53]: frame2['eastern'] = frame2.state == 'Ohio'

In [54]: frame2

Out[54]:

 year state pop debt eastern

one 2000 Ohio 1.5 NaN True

two 2001 Ohio 1.7 -1.2 True

three 2002 Ohio 3.6 NaN True

four 2001 Nevada 2.4 -1.5 False

five 2002 Nevada 2.9 -1.7 False

In [55]: del frame2['eastern']

In [56]: frame2.columns

Out[56]: Index([year, state, pop, debt], dtype=object)

A nested dict of dicts format is another common form of data:

In [57]: pop = {'Nevada': {2001: 2.4, 2002: 2.9},

....: 'Ohio': {2000: 1.5, 2001: 1.7, 2002: 3.6}}

If it is passed the DataFrame, the outer dict keys will be interpreted as they enter keys and columns as the row indices:

In [58]: frame3 = DataFrame(pop)

In [59]: frame3

Out[59]:

 Nevada Ohio

2000 NaN 1.5

2001 2.4 1.7

2002 2.9 3.6

Of course, the result can always be transposed:

In [60]: frame3.T

Out[60]:

 2000 2001 2002

Nevada NaN 2.4 2.9

Ohio 1.5 1.7 3.6

The inner dicts keys are sorted and unioned to form the index as a result. Though this isn't necessarily true if an explicit index has been specified:

In [61]: DataFrame(pop, index=[2001, 2002, 2003])

Out[61]:

 Nevada Ohio

2001 2.4 1.7

2002 2.9 3.6

2003 NaN

Series dicts are treated in a similar manner:

In [62]: pdata = {'Ohio': frame3['Ohio'][:-1],

....: 'Nevada': frame3['Nevada'][:2]}

In [63]: DataFrame(pdata)

Out[63]:

 Nevada Ohio

2000 NaN 1.5

2001 2.4 1.7

If the columns and index of a DataFrame have had their name attributes set, the following will be displayed:

In [64]: frame3.index.name = 'year'; frame3.columns.name = 'state'

In [65]: frame3

Out[65]:

state Nevada Ohio

year

2000 NaN 1.5

2001 2.4 1.7

2002 2.9 3.6

Similar to Series, the attribute of values will have the data contained in the DataFrame returned as a 2D ndarray:

In [66]: frame3.values

Out[66]:

array([[nan, 1.5],

[2.4, 1.7],

[2.9, 3.6]])

The columns of the DataFrame are of different dtypes, the values array the type selected to accommodate every column:

In [67]: frame2.values

Out[67]:

array([[2000, Ohio, 1.5, nan],

[2001, Ohio, 1.7, -1.2],

[2002, Ohio, 3.6, nan],

[2001, Nevada, 2.4, -1.5],

[2002, Nevada, 2.9, -1.7]], dtype=object)

Series

A Pandas Series is an index data of one-dimensional array. It is usually created from a list or array as shown below:

In[2]: data = pd.Series([0.25, 0.5, 0.75, 1.0])

data

Out[2]: 0 0.25

1 0.50

2 0.75

3 1.00

dtype: float64

As in the output above, the Series wraps both a sequence of indices and a sequence of values, that we can access with index and values attributes. The values are basically a familiar NumPy array:

In[3]: data.values

Out[3]: array([0.25, 0.5 , 0.75, 1.])

The index is an array type of object belonging to pd.Index:

In[4]: data.index

Out[4]: RangeIndex(start=0, stop=4, step=1)

As with a NumPy array, use the associate index to access data via the familiar Python square-bracket notation:

In[5]: data[1]

Out[5]: 0.5

In[6]: data[1:3]

Out[6]: 1 0.50

2 0.75

dtype: float64

As we come across, the Pandas Series is way more flexible in general than the one-dimensional NumPy array that it emulates.

Series As Specialized Dictionary

Let's take a Pandas Series as a specialization of a Python dictionary.

Over here, a dictionary is a structure in which arbitrary keys has been mapped to a group of arbitrary values, whereas a Series is a structure where typed keys are mapped to a group of typed values. This kind of typing is essential: similar to how more efficient the type-specific code compiled behind a NumPy array is then a Python list for particular functions, a Pandas Series' type information is more efficient than Python dictionaries for particular functions.

Let's construct a Series object straight from a Python dictionary to give the Series-as-dictionary analogy more clarity:

In[11]: population_dict = {'California': 38332521,

'Texas': 26448193,

'New York': 19651127,

'Florida': 19552860,

'Illinois': 12882135}

population = pd.Series(population_dict)

population

Out[11]: California 38332521

Florida 19552860

Illinois 12882135

New York 19651127

Texas 26448193

dtype: int64

A Series where the index has been drawn from the sorted keys will be created by default. From this point, a typical dictionary-type item access can be done:

In[12]: population['California']

Out[12]: 38332521

However, unlike a dictionary, the Series can also support array-style functions like slicing:

In[13]: population['California':'Illinois']

Out[13]: California 38332521

Florida 19552860

Illinois 12882135

dtype: int64

Generalized NumPy Array Series

It may seem as if the object of Series is the same as a NumPy array of one-dimension. The only difference, however, is how the index is presented: whereas the NumPy array as an integer index that is implicitly defined that allows us to access values, the Panda Series consists of an index more explicitly defined that is linked with values.

Because of this, the Series object is given several capabilities. For instance, instead of being an integer, an index can have values of any preferred type. Strings can be used as an index, for example:

In[7]: data = pd.Series([0.25, 0.5, 0.75, 1.0],

index=['a', 'b', 'c', 'd'])

data

Out[7]: a 0.25

b 0.50

c 0.75

d 1.00

dtype: float64

With this, item access can work as we expect it to:

In[8]: data['b']

Out[8]: 0.5

We can also use nonsequential or noncontiguous indices:

In[9]: data = pd.Series([0.25, 0.5, 0.75, 1.0],

index=[2, 5, 3, 7])

data

Out[9]: 2 0.25

5 0.50

3 0.75

7 1.00

dtype: float64

In[10]: data[5]

Out[10]: 0.5

Making Series Objects

We've already seen how a Panda Series can be constructed from scratch in several ways; all of which have some iteration of the following:

>>> pd.Series(data, index=index)

In this, an index is an optional argument, and data may be one of several other entities.

Data, for example, may either be a list or NumPy array, which in this case, the index could default to a sequence of integers.

In[14]: pd.Series([2, 4, 6])

Out[14]: 0 2

1 4

2 6

dtype: int64

Data can be a scalar, which fills the specified index when repeated:

In[15]: pd.Series(5, index=[100, 200, 300])

Out[15]: 100 5

200 5

300 5

dtype: int64

Data may be a dictionary, where index would be defaulted to the sorted dictionary keys:

In[16]: pd.Series({2:'a', 1:'b', 3:'c'})

Out[16]: 1 b

2 a

3 c

dtype: object

In every case, the index can be set explicitly if different results are preferred:

In[17]: pd.Series({2:'a', 1:'b', 3:'c'}, index=[3, 2])

Out[17]: 3 c

2 a

dtype: object

If you look closely, the Series only populated with only those keys that have been explicitly identified.

Pandas Index Object

We've seen how objects from both DataFrame and Series consist of an explicit index that allows you to modify and reference data. The Index object is itself is an interesting structure that can be assumed as an ordered set or an immutable array. These views come with interesting consequences in the functions available on Index objects. Let's try to construct an Index from a list of integers:

```
In[30]: ind = pd.Index([2, 3, 5, 7, 11])

ind

Out[30]: Int64Index([2, 3, 5, 7, 11], dtype='int64')
```

Index As Ordered Set

Objects from pandas are made for operations like joins across data sets, which depends on several set arithmetic aspects. The Index object follows many of the Python's built-in set data structure conventions, just so intersections, differences, unions, as well as other combinations can be computed in a similar manner:

```
In[35]: indA = pd.Index([1, 3, 5, 7, 9])

indB = pd.Index([2, 3, 5, 7, 11])

In[36]: indA & indB # intersection

Out[36]: Int64Index([3, 5, 7], dtype='int64')

In[37]: indA | indB # union

Out[37]: Int64Index([1, 2, 3, 5, 7, 9, 11], dtype='int64')

In[38]: indA ^ indB # symmetric difference

Out[38]: Int64Index([1, 2, 9, 11], dtype='int64')
```

These operations can also be accessed through object methods such asindA.intersection(indB).

Index As Immutable Array

In many ways, the Index object works like an array. For instance, the standard Python indexing notation can be used to retrieve slices or values:

In[31]: ind[1]

Out[31]: 3

In[32]: ind[::2]

Out[32]: Int64Index([2, 5, 11], dtype='int64')

Index objects also share numerous NumPy array attributes that may be familiar to users:

In[33]: print(ind.size, ind.shape, ind.ndim, ind.dtype)

5 (5,) 1 int64

The difference between NumPy arrays and Index objects is that indices are immutable – which means they can't be modified through normal means:

In[34]: ind[1] = 0

TypeError Traceback (most recent call last)

<ipython-input-34-40e631c82e8a> in <module>()

----> 1 ind[1] = 0

/Users/jakevdp/anaconda/lib/python3.5/site-packages/pandas/indexes/base.py ...

1243

1244 def __setitem__(self, key, value):

-> 1245 raise TypeError("Index does not support mutable operations")

1246

1247 def __getitem__(self, key):

TypeError: Index does not support mutable operations

The immutability enables the sharing of indices between several arrays and DataFrames safer without any potential side effects from inadvertent index modification.

Essential Functionality

Over here, we'll go over the basic mechanics of interacting with data stored in a DataFrame or a Series. We'll also delve deeper into data manipulation and analysis topics with the use of pandas.

Reindexing

Re-index is a critical method on pandas, in which a new object is created using data conformed to a new index. Consider the example as follows:

n [79]: obj = Series([4.5, 7.2, -5.3, 3.6], index=['d', 'b', 'a', 'c'])

In [80]: obj

Out[80]:

d 4.5

b 7.2

a -5.3

c 3.6

If you call a reindex on this Series, the data will be rearranged to the new index, were missing values any index values that were not previously there will be introduced:

In [81]: obj2 = obj.reindex(['a', 'b', 'c', 'd', 'e'])

In [82]: obj2

Out[82]:

a -5.3

b 7.2

c 3.6

d 4.5

e NaN

In [83]: obj.reindex(['a', 'b', 'c', 'd', 'e'], fill_value=0)

Out[83]:

a -5.3

b 7.2

c 3.6

d 4.5

e 0.0

For ordered data such as the time series, it may be better to fill or interpolate values when reindexing. This can be accomplished using the method option, in which methods like ffill fills values:

In [84]: obj3 = Series(['blue', 'purple', 'yellow'], index=[0, 2, 4])

In [85]: obj3.reindex(range(6), method='ffill')

Out[85]:

0 blue

1 blue

2 purple

3 purple

4 yellow

5 yellow

Using DataFrame, reindex could change columns, (row) index, or perhaps even both. When a sequence has been passed, the rows will be reindexed as follows:

In [86]: frame = DataFrame(np.arange(9).reshape((3, 3)), index=['a', 'c', 'd'],

.....: columns=['Ohio', 'Texas', 'California'])

In [87]: frame

Out[87]:

 Ohio Texas California

a 0 1 2

c 3 4 5

d 6 7 8

In [88]: frame2 = frame.reindex(['a', 'b', 'c', 'd'])

In [89]: frame2

Out[89]:

Ohio Texas California

a 0 1 2

b NaN NaN NaN

c 3 4 5

d 6 7 8

The columns keyword allows you to reindex the columns:

In [90]: states = ['Texas', 'Utah', 'California']

In [91]: frame.reindex(columns=states)

Out[91]:

 Texas Utah California

a 1 NaN 2

c 4 NaN 5

d 7 NaN 8

Both of them can be reindexed in one go, although interpellation applies row-wise only:

In [92]: frame.reindex(index=['a', 'b', 'c', 'd'], method='ffill',

....: columns=states)

Out[92]:

Texas Utah California

a 1 NaN 2

b 1 NaN 2

c 4 NaN 5

d 7 NaN 8

As you see the results that follow, reindexing can be done clearly by label-indexing with ix:

In [93]: frame.ix[['a', 'b', 'c', 'd'], states]

Out[93]:

Texas Utah California

a 1 NaN 2

b NaN NaN NaN

c 4 NaN 5

d 7 NaN 8

Indexing, Selection, and Filtering

Series indexing such as obj [...] In the same manner as NumPy array indexing, but instead of using only integers, you can use the Series's index values. Some examples of this include:

In [102]: obj = Series(np.arange(4.), index=['a', 'b', 'c', 'd'])

In [103]: obj['b'] In [104]: obj[1]

Out[103]: 1.0 Out[104]: 1.0

In [105]: obj[2:4] In [106]: obj[['b', 'a', 'd']]

Out[105]: Out[106]:

c 2 b 1

d 3 a 0

　 d 3

In [107]: obj[[1, 3]] In [108]: obj[obj < 2]

Out[107]: Out[108]:

b 1 a 0

d 3 b 1

Label slicing is different than regular Python slicing in which the endpoint is inclusive:

In [109]: obj['b':'c']

Out[109]:

b 1

c 2

Using setting with these methods works just as one would expect:

In [110]: obj['b':'c'] = 5

In [111]: obj

Out[111]:

a 0

b 5

c 5

d 3

As you've seen, indexing and with DataFrame helps users retrieve one or more columns either with a single value or sequence of values:

In [112]: data = DataFrame(np.arange(16).reshape((4, 4)),

.....: index=['Ohio', 'Colorado', 'Utah', 'New York'],

.....: columns=['one', 'two', 'three', 'four'])

In [113]: data

Out[113]:

 one two three four

Ohio 0 1 2 3

Colorado 4 5 6 7

Utah 8 9 10 11

New York 12 13 14 15

In [114]: data['two'] In [115]: data[['three', 'one']]

Out[114]: Out[115]:

Ohio 1 three one

Colorado 5 Ohio 2 0

Utah 9 Colorado 6 4

New York 13 Utah 10 8

Name: two New York 14 12

Indexing in this manner has a couple of special cases. The first is when roles are selected by a Boolean array or slicing:

In [116]: data[:2] In [117]: data[data['three'] > 5]

Out[116]: Out[117]:

one two three four one two three four

Ohio 0 1 2 3 Colorado 4 5 6 7

Colorado 4 5 6 7 Utah 8 9 10 11

New York 12 13 14 15

Some readers may find this to be inconsistent, but the syntax came from practicality and nothing else. Another case would be in indexing using a Boolean DataFrame, like the one developed using a scalar comparison,

In [118]: data < 5

Out[118]:

 one two three four

Ohio True True True True

Colorado True False False False

Utah False False False False

New York False False False False

In [119]: data[data < 5] = 0

In [120]: data

Out[120]:

 one two three four

Ohio 0 0 0 0

Colorado 0 5 6 7

Utah 8 9 10 11

New York 12 13 14 15

This synthetically makes DataFrame more like an ndarray.

For DataFrame row label-indexing, let's introduce special indexing field ix. You can choose a subset of the columns and rows from a DataFrame with NumPy-like notation plus axis labels:

```
In [121]: data.ix['Colorado', ['two', 'three']]

Out[121]:

two 5

three 6

Name: Colorado

In [122]: data.ix[['Colorado', 'Utah'], [3, 0, 1]]

Out[122]:

 four one two

Colorado 7 0 5

Utah 11 8 9

In [123]: data.ix[2] In [124]: data.ix[:'Utah', 'two']

Out[123]: Out[124]:

one 8 Ohio 0

two 9 Colorado 5

three 10 Utah 9

four 11 Name: two

Name: Utah


In [125]: data.ix[data.three > 5, :3]
```

Out[125]:

one two three

Colorado 0 5 6

Utah 8 9 10

New York 12 13 14

So as you can see, there are several ways to choose and rearrange data stored in a pandas object.

How to Drop Entries from an Axis

It's easy to drop one or several other entries from an access once you have an index array or list without any of those entries. Seeing as how that requires of bit of set logic and munging, the method drop returns a new object with the indicated value or values that were deleted from an axis:

In [94]: obj = Series(np.arange(5.), index=['a', 'b', 'c', 'd', 'e'])

In [95]: new_obj = obj.drop('c')

In [96]: new_obj

Out[96]:

a 0

b 1

d 3

e 4

In [97]: obj.drop(['d', 'c'])

Out[97]:

a 0

b 1

e 4

Using DataFrame, you can delete index values from either access:

In [98]: data = DataFrame(np.arange(16).reshape((4, 4)),

....: index=['Ohio', 'Colorado', 'Utah', 'New York'],

....: columns=['one', 'two', 'three', 'four'])

In [99]: data.drop(['Colorado', 'Ohio'])

Out[99]:

 one two three four

Utah 8 9 10 11

New York 12 13 14 15

In [100]: data.drop('two', axis=1) In [101]: data.drop(['two', 'four'], axis=1)

Out[100]: Out[101]:

 one three four one three

Ohio 0 2 3 Ohio 0 2

Colorado 4 6 7 Colorado 4 6

Utah 8 10 11 Utah 8 10

New York 12 14 15 New York 12 14

Function Application and Mapping

NumPy ufuncs work well with pandas objects:

In [158]: frame = DataFrame(np.random.randn(4, 3), columns=list('bde'),

.....: index=['Utah', 'Ohio', 'Texas', 'Oregon'])

In [159]: frame In [160]: np.abs(frame)

Out[159]: Out[160]:

b d e b d e

Utah -0.204708 0.478943 -0.519439 Utah 0.204708 0.478943 0.519439

Ohio -0.555730 1.965781 1.393406 Ohio 0.555730 1.965781 1.393406

Texas 0.092908 0.281746 0.769023 Texas 0.092908 0.281746 0.769023

Oregon 1.246435 1.007189 -1.296221 Oregon 1.246435 1.007189 1.296221

Another usual operation is when a function on 1D arrays have been applied to each row or column. The apply method from DataFrame does the following:

In [161]: f = lambda x: x.max() - x.min()

In [162]: frame.apply(f) In [163]: frame.apply(f, axis=1)

71

Out[162]: Out[163]:

b 1.802165 Utah 0.998382

d 1.684034 Ohio 2.521511

e 2.689627 Texas 0.676115

Many array statistics (such as mean and sum) are data frame methods, so it's not necessary to apply them.

A scalar value is not returned after the function is passed to apply. It can even return a Series with several values:

In [164]: def f(x):

.....: return Series([x.min(), x.max()], index=['min', 'max'])

In [165]: frame.apply(f)

Out[165]:

 b d e

min -0.555730 0.281746 -1.296221

max 1.246435 1.965781 1.393406

You can also use element-wise Python functions. Let's say you want a formatted string computed from each of the frame's floating point values. We can use applymap to do this:

In [166]: format = lambda x: '%.2f' % x

In [167]: frame.applymap(format)

Out[167]:

b d e

Utah -0.20 0.48 -0.52

Ohio -0.56 1.97 1.39

Texas 0.09 0.28 0.77

Oregon 1.25 1.01 -1.30

The reason for the applymap name is that Series can apply an element-wise function with a map method:

In [168]: frame['e'].map(format)

Out[168]:

Utah -0.52

Ohio 1.39

Texas 0.77

Oregon -1.30

Name: e

Arithmetic and Data Alignment

The behavior of arithmetic between objects with varying indexes is one of the most crucial pandas features. When objects are added together, should any index pair not be the same, the index in the result will be the union of the index pairs. Let's take a simple example like this one:

In [126]: s1 = Series([7.3, -2.5, 3.4, 1.5], index=['a', 'c', 'd', 'e'])

In [127]: s2 = Series([-2.1, 3.6, -1.5, 4, 3.1], index=['a', 'c', 'e', 'f', 'g'])

In [128]: s1 In [129]: s2

Out[128]: Out[129]:

a 7.3 a -2.1

c -2.5 c 3.6

d 3.4 e -1.5

e 1.5 f 4.0

  g 3.1

Adding them together brings us:

In [130]: s1 + s2

Out[130]:

a 5.2

c 1.1

d NaN

e 0.0

f NaN

g NaN

The internal data alignment brings NA values in indices that don't overlap. Missing values grow in arithmetic computations.

When it comes to DataFrame, alignment is performed on both the columns and the rows:

In [131]: df1 = DataFrame(np.arange(9.).reshape((3, 3)), columns=list('bcd'),

.....: index=['Ohio', 'Texas', 'Colorado'])

In [132]: df2 = DataFrame(np.arange(12.).reshape((4, 3)), columns=list('bde'),

.....: index=['Utah', 'Ohio', 'Texas', 'Oregon'])

In [133]: df1 In [134]: df2

Out[133]: Out[134]:

b c d b d e

Ohio 0 1 2 Utah 0 1 2

Texas 3 4 5 Ohio 3 4 5

Colorado 6 7 8 Texas 6 7 8

Oregon 9 10 11

Adding these together returns a DataFrame whose index and columns are the unions of the ones in each DataFrame:

In [135]: df1 + df2

Out[135]:

b c d e

Colorado NaN NaN NaN NaN

Ohio 3 NaN 6 NaN

Oregon NaN NaN NaN NaN

Texas 9 NaN 12 NaN

Utah NaN NaN NaN NaN

Operations Between Series and DataFrame

Similar to NumPy arrays, arithmetic between Series and DataFrame is well-defined. First, you should consider the difference between a 2D array and one of its rows:

In [143]: arr = np.arange(12.).reshape((3, 4))

In [144]: arr

Out[144]:

array([[0., 1., 2., 3.],

 [4., 5., 6., 7.],

 [8., 9., 10., 11.]])

In [145]: arr[0]

Out[145]: array([0., 1., 2., 3.])

In [146]: arr - arr[0]

Out[146]:

array([[0., 0., 0., 0.],

 [4., 4., 4., 4.],

 [8., 8., 8., 8.]])

Operations between a Series and a DataFrame are similar:

In [147]: frame = DataFrame(np.arange(12.).reshape((4, 3)), columns=list('bde'),

.....: index=['Utah', 'Ohio', 'Texas', 'Oregon'])

In [148]: series = frame.ix[0]

In [149]: frame In [150]: series

Out[149]: Out[150]:

b d e b 0

Utah 0 1 2 d 1

Ohio 3 4 5 e 2

Texas 6 7 8 Name: Utah

Oregon 9 10 11

Arithmetic between Series and DataFrame match the Series index on the columns of the DataFrame, broadcasting down the rows:

In [151]: frame - series

Out[151]:

b d e

Utah 0 0 0

Ohio 3 3 3

Texas 6 6 6

Oregon 9 9 9

If an index value isn't found in either the Series's index or the columns of the DataFrame, the objects will be reindexed to form the union:

In [152]: series2 = Series(range(3), index=['b', 'e', 'f'])

In [153]: frame + series2

Out[153]:

b d e f

Utah 0 NaN 3 NaN

Ohio 3 NaN 6 NaN

Texas 6 NaN 9 NaN

Oregon 9 NaN 12 NaN

If you wish to broadcast over the columns that match on the rows instead, you have to use one of the recommended methods. For example:

In [154]: series3 = frame['d']

In [155]: frame In [156]: series3

Out[155]: Out[156]:

b d e Utah 1

Utah 0 1 2 Ohio 4

Ohio 3 4 5 Texas 7

Texas 6 7 8 Oregon 10

Oregon 9 10 11 Name: d

In [157]: frame.sub(series3, axis=0)

Out[157]:

b d e

Utah -1 0 1

Ohio -1 0 1

Texas -1 0 1

Oregon -1 0 1

The axis number that you be passing is the axis to match on. For this, we match on the DataFrames row index and broadcast across.

Arithmetic Methods with Fill Values

Arithmetic operations involving objects of varying indexes might want you to fill it with a special value, such as 0, when there is an axle label in one object and not the other:

In [136]: df1 = DataFrame(np.arange(12.).reshape((3, 4)), columns=list('abcd'))

In [137]: df2 = DataFrame(np.arange(20.).reshape((4, 5)), columns=list('abcde'))

In [138]: df1 In [139]: df2

Out[138]: Out[139]:

a b c d a b c d e

0 0 1 2 3 0 0 1 2 3 4

1 4 5 6 7 1 5 6 7 8 9

2 8 9 10 11 2 10 11 12 13 14

3 15 16 17 18 19

When these are added in NA values in areas that don't overlap:

In [140]: df1 + df2

Out[140]:

 a b c d e

0 0 2 4 6 NaN

1 9 11 13 15 NaN

2 18 20 22 24 NaN

3 NaN NaN NaN NaN NaN

When the add method on df1 is used, df2 should be passed an argument to fill_value:

In [141]: df1.add(df2, fill_value=0)

Out[141]:

 a b c d e

0 0 2 4 6 4

1 9 11 13 15 9

2 18 20 22 24 14

3 15 16 17 18 19

Similarly, when a DataFrame or Series has been re-indexed, a different fill value can be specified:

In [142]: df1.reindex(columns=df2.columns, fill_value=0)

Out[142]:

 a b c d e

0 0 1 2 3 0

1 4 5 6 7 0

2 8 9 10 11 0

Sorting and Ranking

Sorting data sets by some criterion is another essential built-in operation. To sort lexicographically by column or row index, you should use the sort_index method, which returns a new, sorted object:

In [169]: obj = Series(range(4), index=['d', 'a', 'b', 'c'])

In [170]: obj.sort_index()

Out[170]:

a 1

b 2

c 3

d 0

With the use of a DataFrame, you can sort using either axis or index:

In [171]: frame = DataFrame(np.arange(8).reshape((2, 4))),
index=['three', 'one'],

.....: columns=['d', 'a', 'b', 'c'])

In [172]: frame.sort_index() In [173]:
frame.sort_index(axis=1)

Out[172]: Out[173]:

d a b c a b c d

one 4 5 6 7 three 1 2 3 0

three 0 1 2 3 one 5 6 7 4

By default, data is sorted in ascending order, but can also be done in ascending order as well:

In [174]: frame.sort_index(axis=1, ascending=False)

Out[174]:

d c b a

three 0 3 2 1

one 4 7 6 5

The order method can be used to sort a Series by its values:

In [175]: obj = Series([4, 7, -3, 2])

In [176]: obj.order()

Out[176]:

2 -3

3 2

0 4

1 7

By default, any missing values will be sorted to the end of the Series:

In [177]: obj = Series([4, np.nan, 7, np.nan, -3, 2])

In [178]: obj.order()

Out[178]:

4 -3

5 2

0 4

2 7

1 NaN

3 NaN

When using DataFrame, you should sort by values and one or more columns. To do that, you can pass one or more column names to the by option:

In [179]: frame = DataFrame({'b': [4, 7, -3, 2], 'a': [0, 1, 0, 1]})

In [180]: frame In [181]: frame.sort_index(by='b')

Out[180]: Out[181]:

a b a b

0 0 4 2 0 -3

1 1 7 3 1 2

2 0 -3 0 0 4

3 1 2 1 1 7

You can pass a list of names to sort by multiple columns:

In [182]: frame.sort_index(by=['a', 'b'])

Out[182]:

 a b

2 0 -3

0 0 4

3 1 2

1 1 7

Ranking can be closely linked to sorting, which is when ranks are assigned from one through a number of valid array data points. This is identical to the indirect sort indices made from numpy. argsort, except these ties, are broken due to a rule. You should look at the rank methods for DataFrame and Series; the ties are broken by rank when each group has been assigned the mean rank by default:

In [183]: obj = Series([7, -5, 7, 4, 2, 0, 4])

In [184]: obj.rank()

Out[184]:

0 6.5

1 1.0

2 6.5

3 4.5

4 3.0

5 2.0

6 4.5

Ranks can even be assigned in the order that they are observed in the data:

In [185]: obj.rank(method='first')

Out[185]:

0 6

1 1

2 7

3 4

4 3

5 2

6 5

They can also be ranked in descending order as well:

In [186]: obj.rank(ascending=False, method='max')

Out[186]:

0 2

1 7

2 2

3 4

4 5

5 6

6 4

Ranks can be computed by DataFrames over the columns or rows:

In [187]: frame = DataFrame({'b': [4.3, 7, -3, 2], 'a': [0, 1, 0, 1],

.....: 'c': [-2, 5, 8, -2.5]})

In [188]: frame In [189]: frame.rank(axis=1)

Out[188]: Out[189]:

 a b c a b c

0 0 4.3 -2.0 0 2 3 1

1 1 7.0 5.0 1 1 3 2

2 0 -3.0 8.0 2 2 1 3

3 1 2.0 -2.5 3 2 3 1

Axis Indexes with Duplicate Values

As of now, every example that we shared with you has had unique axis labels. Whereas most pandas functions (such as **reindex**) require unique labels, it's not really important. Let's take a small Series with duplicate indices:

In [190]: obj = Series(range(5), index=['a', 'a', 'b', 'b', 'c'])

In [191]: obj

Out[191]:

a 0

a 1

b 2

b 3

c 4

The is_unique property let you know whether the values are unique or not:

In [192]: obj.index.is_unique

Out[192]: False

One of the things that behave differently with duplicates is data selection. Indexing values with various entries will have a Series returned whereas single entries will have a scalar value returned:

In [193]: obj['a'] In [194]: obj['c']

Out[193]: Out[194]: 4

a 0

a 1

The same concept applies to indexing DataFrame rows:

```
In [195]: df = DataFrame(np.random.randn(4, 3), index=['a',
'a', 'b', 'b'])

In [196]: df
Out[196]:
 0 1 2
a 0.274992 0.228913 1.352917
a 0.886429 -2.001637 -0.371843
b 1.669025 -0.438570 -0.539741
b 0.476985 3.248944 -1.021228

In [197]: df.ix['b']
Out[197]:
 0 1 2
b 1.669025 -0.438570 -0.539741
b 0.476985 3.248944 -1.021228
```

Chapter Three

How to Get Started with Raw Data

Raw data can come in a variety of forms and sizes in the data science ecosystem. There is plenty of information from within raw data that can be extracted and used in several ways. For example, the global online retailer Amazon gathers up clickstream data which records a visitor's click on their website. The company then analyzes this data to determine if a user is either price-sensitive or prefers products that are more highly reviewed and rated. If you are an Amazon regular, you must've noticed a panel of recommended products on the website; this is derived from data of customers who visit the site often.

The first thing you need to know to make sense of such an analysis is to parse raw data. For data parsing, you need to utilize the steps provided below:

- **Extract data from the source:** data has many forms including CSV, Excel, databases, JSON and more. And with the help of some useful packages – which we will cover later on – Python will make it easier for you to read data from these sources.

- **Cleaning data:** after a sanity check has been performed, data needs to be cleaned properly before it can be utilized for analysis. You might have a data set about members of the police station, including details about their weight, height, as well as their daily duties. You might find that there could be certain rows in which the weight and height details are missing. As such, the rows that have missing values will either be ignored or replaced with the average weight or height, depending on how the analysis is being performed.

The following topics will be covered in this chapter:

- How to use pandas to handle data

- How to explore arrays with NumPy

- How to handle missing data

- How to read and write data from various formats

- How to manipulate data

Using Pandas for Data Analysis

The pandas library, developed by Wes McKinney, is an open-source Python library designed especially for data analysis. It was built on NumPy and makes handling data easy. NumPy is a low-level tool that makes handling matrices really good.

The pandas library utilizes the power of R when it comes to handling data. Thanks to its sufficient data structures, it is able to perform fast joins, process data, and read data several sources, among so many other functions.

Pandas Data Structure

The pandas library comprise the three data structures, including:

1. DataFrame

2. Series

3. Panel

DataFrame

DataFrame is into the data structure that comprises of columns of varying data types. It can be viewed as a table. Users can form DataFrame using the following data structures:

- Lists

- a NumPy array

- Series

- Dicts

- a 2D NumPy array

You can use the commands below to create a DataFrame from a dict of series:

>>> d = {'c1': pd.Series(['A', 'B', 'C']),

'c2': pd.Series([1, 2., 3., 4.])}

>>> df = pd.DataFrame(d)

>>> df

c1 c2

0 A 1

1 B 2

2 C 3

3 NaN 4

A dict of lists can also be used to create a DataFrame:

```
>>> d = {'c1': ['A', 'B', 'C', 'D'],   'c2': [1, 2.0, 3.0, 4.0]}

>>> df = pd.DataFrame(d)

>>> print df

c1  c2

0 A  1

1 B  2

2 C  3

3 D  4
```

Panel

A panel is a data structure responsible for handling 3D data. An example of the panel data is:

```
>>> d = {'Item1': pd.DataFrame(np.random.randn(4, 3)),

'Item2': pd.DataFrame(np.random.randn(4, 2))}

>>> pd.Panel(d)



<class 'pandas.core.panel.Panel'>
```

Dimensions: 2 (items) x 4 (major_axis) x 3 (minor_axis)Items axis: Item1 to Item2

```
Major_axis axis: 0 to 3

Minor_axis axis: 0 to 2
```

The command shown above reveals two items representing 2 DataFrames. Four major axes represent four rows and three minor axes that represent three columns.

Series

Series is a one-dimensional array that can hold various types of data such as floats, integers, strings as well as Python objects. You can create a series using the following code:

```
>>> import pandas as pd

>>> pd.Series(np.random.randn(5))

0       0.733810

1       -1.274658

2       -1.602298

3       0.460944

4       -0.632756

dtype: float64
```

The parameter known as random. randn belongs to the NumPy package were random numbers are generated. The series function produces a pandas series that includes the first column known as an index, and the second column that contains random values. The series datatype lies at the bottom of the output.

Users can customize the series' index by calling the following code:

```
>>> pd.Series(np.random.randn(5), index=['a', 'b', 'c', 'd', 'e'])

a       -0.929494
```

b   -0.571423

c   -1.197866

d   0.081107

e   -0.035091

dtype: float64

A series can also be derived from a Phyton dict:

>>> d = {'A': 10, 'B': 20, 'C': 30}

>>> pd.Series(d)

A   10

B   20

C   30

dtype: int64

Using NumPy to Explore Arrays

By default, Python already comes with a data structure like List, that programmers can use for area operations. However, a Python list will be able to perform complex mathematical operations on its own as it's not optimized for such things.

This is where Travis Oliphant's wonderful Python package, NumPy, comes into play as it has been developed specifically for scientific computing. It is capable of handling enormous multidimensional matrices and arrays, and a huge library of high-level mathematical functions so these arrays can be operated on.

NumPy array doesn't use as much memory to store the same amount of data in a Python list, which makes reading and writing from the array easier and faster.

How to Create an Array

To create a NumPy array object, a list of numbers has to be passed to the following array function:

>>> import numpy as np

>>> n_array = np.array([[0, 1, 2, 3],

[4, 5, 6, 7],

[8, 9, 10, 11]])

There are several attributes in a NumPy array object that can aid in providing information about the array, including:

- Shape: which gives each of the array's dimension its size:

>>> n_array.shape

(3, 4)

The first dimension denoted by n-array has a size 3 to it, and the second dimension has 4. This means it has three rows and four columns.

- ndim: this represents the number of dimensions there are in an array. For example, the following array has two dimensions which are shown as:

>>> n_array.ndim

2

The 2 in n_array represents its rank, indicating it to be a 2D array.

- dtype: the elements in the array are given a datatype:

    >>> n_array.dtype.name

    int64

this number is stored as int64 in n_array.

- size: the number of elements is given here:

    >>> n_array.size

    12

In the code above, the total number of elements is 12.

Performing Mathematical Operations

Certain mathematical operations have to be performed on an array of data. Let's discuss a couple of them in the sections that follow.

Subtraction in an Array

Using the command as follows, you will be subtracting the 'a' array from the 'b' array to get the 'c' array. The subtraction occurs one element at a time:

    >>> a = np.array([11, 12, 13, 14])

    >>> b = np.array([1, 2, 3, 4])

    >>> c = a - b

    >>>c

    Array[10 10 10 10]

Just remember that when you subtract two arrays, both of them should have equal dimensions.

Squaring

An element can be raised to the power of two using the following command:

>>> b**2

[1 4 9 16

Trigonometric Function

The command below gives each of the 'b' array's values cosine to obtain the desired result:

>>> np.cos(b)

[0.54030231 -0.41614684 -0.9899925 -0.65364362]

Matrix Multiplication

Two matrices can be multiplied in a dot product or one element at a time. The command below performs the dot product multiplication:

>>> np.dot(A1, A2)

[[5 4]

[3 4]]

Element-by-element multiplication can be performed as follows:

>>> A1 = np.array([[1, 1],

[0, 1]])

>>> A2 = np.array([[2, 0],

[3, 4]])


```
>>> A1 * A2
```

[[2 0]

[0 4]]

Conditional Operations

To generate the respective Boolean values, the command below applies the conditional operation to each of the 'b' array's elements;

```
>>> b<2
```

[True False False False]

Manipulating Shape

After it has been created, the shape of an array can be changed as well. If you want to flatten the array, use the following command:

```
>>> n_array.ravel()
```

[0 1 2 3 4 5 6 7 8 9 10 11]

The command below will shape the array in a format of six rows and two columns. And during the time of reshaping, you will see that the new shape has to have the same number of elements as the one before:

```
>>> n_array.shape = (6,2)
```

```
>>> n_array
```

[[0 1]

[2 3]

[4 5]

[6 7]

[8 9]

[10 11]]

You can also transpose the array:

>>> n_array.transpose()

[[0 2 4 6 8 10]

[1 3 5 7 9 11]]

How to Insert and Export Data

Data can be stored in several forms, including TSV, CSV, databases and more. It's really convenient to read data of each of those formats from the panda's library or even export data to these formats. You'll be needing a database that consists of the weight statistics of police officers from all over the country.

You'll need a file with the structure as follows:

Column	Description
COUNTY	The county that the police station belongs to
LOCATION CODE	Unique location code
REGION	The region the police station belongs to

AREA NAME	The district that the police station belongs to
PCT OVERWEIGHT	The percentage of overweight officers
NO. OVERWEIGHT	The number of overweight officers
STATION YEARS	The station year being addressed in the data
PCT OBESE	The percentage of obese officers
NO. OBESE	The number of obese officers
PCT OVERWEIGHT OR OBESE	The percentage of officers who are obese or overweight
NO. OVERWEIGHT OR OBESE	The number of officers who are overweight or obese
CITY	The city the police station belongs to
STREET ADDRESS	The address of the police station
AREA TYPE	The type of area
RANK LEVEL	Whether they are high- or low-ranking officers
STATE	The state the police station belongs to

ZIP CODE	The ZIP Code of the police station
LOCATION 1	The address along with latitude and longitude

CSV

Use the following read_csv function to read data from a .csv file:

```
>>> d =
pd.read_csv('Data/Officer_Weight_Status_Category_
Reporting_Results__Beginning_2010.csv')

>>> d[0:5]['AREA NAME'
```

0   RAVENA COEYMANS SELKIRK CENTRAL POLICE DISTRICT

1   1 RAVENA COEYMANS SELKIRK CENTRAL POLICE DISTRICT

2   2 RAVENA COEYMANS SELKIRK CENTRAL POLICE DISTRICT

3   COHOES CITY POLICE DISTRICT

4   COHOES CITY POLICE DISTRICT

To input the data, the read_csv function will take the .csv file. The command that follows will print the Location column's first five rows.

Use the following to_csv function to write data to the .csv file:

```
>>> d = {'c1': pd.Series(['A', 'B', 'C']),
        'c2': pd.Series([1, 2., 3., 4.])}
>>> df = pd.DataFrame(d)
>>> df.to_csv('sample_data.csv')
```

Using the to_csv method, the DataFrame will be written to a .csv file. The file name and the path where the file will be created has to be mentioned.

JSON

In order to read a JSON file data, you can use Python's standard json package. Reading the file requires the following commands:

```
>>> import json
>>> json_data = open('Data/Officer_Weight_Status_Category
        _Reporting_Results__Beginning_2010.json')
>>> data = json.load(json_data)
>>> json_data.close()
```

The 'open ()' function in the above command will open up a connection to the file. The json.load () function will load the data into Python. And with the json_data.close () function, the connection to the file closes.

You'll also find a function of the pandas library that reads the JSON file, which you can access with pd.read_json ().

XLS

Other than the pandas package, reading an Excel file's data after installing the xlrd package for pandas:

>>> d=pd.read_excel('Data/Officer_Weight_Status_Category _Reporting_Results__Beginning_2010.xls')

This function is identical to the reading commander CSV. If the user wishes to have an Excel file written, will need to install the xlwt package:

>>> df.to_excel('sample_data.xls'

Database

Use the following function to read a database's data:

>>> pd.read_sql_table(table_name, con)

This command will generate a DataFrame. A DataFrame will be returned if an SQLAlchemy engine and a table name had been given. This doesn't support the DBAPI connection. The description of the parameters that were used are as follows:

- con: Referring to the SQLAlchemy engine

- table_name: referring to the SQL table's name in a database

SQL query can be read into a DataFrame with the following command:

>>> pd.read_sql_query(sql, con)

The description of the parameters that were used are as follows:

- con: Referring to the SQLAlchemy engine

- sql: referring to the SQL query that's going to be executed

103

Cleansing Data

In order to analyze raw data or create a dashboard on it, you'll need to clean it. This is so you don't come across any issues with your data afterward. There are several reasons why data could have issues; for instance, there could be a malfunction with the retail shop's point-of-sale system or perhaps some data with missing values were inputted. The following section will teach you how to handle such data.

How to Check for Missing Data

Typically, most data that we deal with are missing some values. There are several reasons why this may be the case: either the data that the source system collects may not have collected those values, or the values never existed in the first place. Once you upload the data, you need to check for missing elements in it. Missing data has to be handled based on the requirements at hand. You can handle missing data by replacing a missing value with an alternative value or by simply removing a row.

In the 'Officer Weight' data, use the following command to see if the location column has any missing value:

>>> d['Location 1'].isnull()

0	False
1	False
2	False
3	False
4	False
5	False
6	False

The notnull () method will output every row as either TRUE or FALSE. If the value is False, then a value is missing. This data can be combined to find the number of times the value has been missing:

>>> d['Location 1'].isnull().value_counts()

False   3246

True   24

dtype: int64

This command shows that the column of Location 1 has over 24 missing value instances. You can handle these values by either having those rows with the missing values removed or have them replaced with some other values. Use the following command to remove the rows:

>>> d = d['Location 1'].dropna()

The command below allows you to remove any row with a missing value instance:

>>> d = d.dropna(how='any')

How to Fill Missing Data

Here are some of the DataFrames that you can work with:

>>> df = pd.DataFrame(np.random.randn(5, 3), index=['a0', 'a10', 'a20', 'a30', 'a40'],

        columns=['X', 'Y', 'Z'])

>>> df

            X   Y   Z

a0	-0.854269	0.117540	1.515373
a10	-0.483923	-0.379934	0.484155
a20	-0.038317	0.196770	-0.564176
a30	0.752686	1.329661	-0.056649
a40	-1.383379	0.632615	1.274481

Now you can add extra row indexes that will create null values in your DataFrame:

```
>>> df2 = df2.reindex(['a0', 'a1', 'a10', 'a11', 'a20', 'a21',
        'a30', 'a31', 'a40', 'a41'])
>>> df2
```

	X	Y	Z
a0	-1.193371	0.912654	-0.780461
a1	NaN	NaN	NaN
a10	1.413044	0.615997	0.947334
a11	NaN	NaN	NaN
a20	1.583516	1.388921	0.458771
a21	NaN	NaN	NaN
a30	0.479579	1.427625	1.407924
a31	NaN	NaN	NaN
a40	0.455510	-0.880937	1.375555
a41	NaN	NaN	NaN

To replace the df2 DataFrame null values with the value zero, you must execute the command given below:

```
>>> df2.fillna(0)
```

	X	Y	Z
a0	-1.193371	0.912654	-0.780461
a1	0.000000	0.000000	0.000000
a10	1.413044	0.615997	0.947334
a11	0.000000	0.000000	0.000000
a20	1.583516	1.388921	0.458771
a21	0.000000	0.000000	0.000000
a30	0.479579	1.427625	1.407924
a31	0.000000	0.000000	0.000000
a40	0.455510	-0.880937	1.375555
a41	0.000000	0.000000	0.000000

If the value has to be filled with forward propagation, meaning the value prior to the column's null value that will be used to fill the null value, you'll need to use the command given below:

```
>>> df2.fillna(method='pad') #filling with forward propagation
```

	X	Y	Z
a0	-1.193371	0.912654	-0.780461
a1	-1.193371	0.912654	-0.780461
a10	1.413044	0.615997	0.947334
a11	1.413044	0.615997	0.947334
a20	1.583516	1.388921	0.458771
a21	1.583516	1.388921	0.458771
a30	0.479579	1.427625	1.407924
a31	0.479579	1.427625	1.407924
a40	0.455510	-0.880937	1.375555
a41	0.455510	-0.880937	1.375555

If you want to fill the null values of those columns with the column mean, then use the command given below:

```
>>> df2.fillna(df2.mean())
```

	X	Y	Z
a0	-1.193371	0.912654	-0.780461
a1	0.547655	0.692852	0.681825
a10	1.413044	0.615997	0.947334
a11	0.547655	0.692852	0.681825

a20	1.583516	1.388921	0.458771
a21	0.547655	0.692852	0.681825
a30	0.479579	1.427625	1.407924
a31	0.547655	0.692852	0.681825
a40	0.455510	-0.880937	1.375555
a41	0.547655	0.692852	0.681825

How to Merge Data

To combine data sets, you need to utilize the pandas' concat function. To do that, take the 'County' and 'Area Name' columns with the first five rows:

>>> d[['AREA NAME', 'COUNTY']][0:5]

	AREA NAME	COUNTY
0	RAVENA COEYMANS SELKIRK CENTRAL POLICE DISTRICT	ALBANY
1	RAVENA COEYMANS SELKIRK CENTRAL POLICE DISTRICT	ALBANY
2	RAVENA COEYMANS SELKIRK CENTRAL POLICE DISTRICT	ALBANY
3	COHOES CITY POLICE DISTRICT	ALBANY
4	COHOES CITY POLICE DISTRICT	ALBANY

Use the following to divide the data:

>>> p1 = d[['AREA NAME', 'COUNTY']][0:2]

>>> p2 = d[['AREA NAME', 'COUNTY']][2:5]

The first two rows are in p1 in the last three are in p2. Using the concat () function, we can combine these pieces:

```
>>> pd.concat([p1,p2])
```

	AREA NAME	COUNTY
0	RAVENA COEYMANS SELKIRK CENTRAL POLICE DISTRICT	ALBANY
1	RAVENA COEYMANS SELKIRK CENTRAL POLICE DISTRICT	ALBANY
2	RAVENA COEYMANS SELKIRK CENTRAL POLICE DISTRICT	ALBANY
3	COHOES CITY POLICE DISTRICT	ALBANY
4	COHOES CITY POLICE DISTRICT	ALBANY

You can assign a key to identify these combined pieces:

```
>>> concatenated = pd.concat([p1,p2], keys = ['p1','p2'])
```

```
>>> concatenated
```

		AREA NAME	COUNTY
p1	0	RAVENA COEYMANS SELKIRK CENTRAL POLICE DISTRICT	ALBANY
	1	RAVENA COEYMANS SELKIRK CENTRAL POLICE DISTRICT	ALBANY
p2	2	RAVENA COEYMANS SELKIRK CENTRAL POLICE DISTRICT	ALBANY

| 3 | COHOES CITY POLICE DISTRICT | ALBANY |

| 4 | COHOES CITY POLICE DISTRICT | ALBANY |

Utilizing the keys, pieces from the concatenated data can be extracted back:

```
>>> concatenated.ix['p1']
```

| | AREA | NAME | COUNTY |

| 0 | RAVEN | COEYMANS SELKIRK CENTRAL POLICE DISTRICT | ALBANY |

| 1 | RAVENA COEYMANS SELKIRK CENTRAL POLICE DISTRICT | | ALBANY |

String Operations

There may come a time where you would have to modify your data's string field column. Some of the string operations are explained in the following technique:

- **Substring:** let's use the first five rows of the data in the column of AREA NAME as the data that we will modify:

```
>>> df = pd.read_csv('Data/Officer
_Weight_Status_Category_
Reporting_Results__Beginning_2010.csv')>>> df['AREA
NAME'][0:5]
```

| 0 | RAVENA COEYMANS SELKIRK CENTRAL POLICE DISTRICT |

| 1 | RAVENA COEYMANS SELKIRK CENTRAL POLICE DISTRICT |

2	RAVENA COEYMANS SELKIRK CENTRAL POLICE DISTRICT
3	COHOES CITY POLICE DISTRICT
4	COHOES CITY POLICE DISTRICT

Name: AREA NAME, dtype: object

If you want to modify the first word from the column of 'Area Name', you can use the 'extract' function as the following command shows:

```
>>> df['AREA NAME'][0:5].str.extract('(\w+)')
```

0	RAVENA
1	RAVENA
2	RAVENA
3	COHOES
4	COHOES

Name: AREA NAME, dtype: object

The 'str' attribute of the series, as shown in the command above, has been utilized. The 'str' class has an 'extract' method, where in order to extract data, a regular and powerful expression could be fed. You can even use it to extract a second word from the AREA NAME column as a separate column:

```
>>> df['AREA NAME'][0:5].str.extract('(\w+)\s(\w+)')
```

	0	1
0	RAVENA	COEYMANS

1	RAVENA	COEYMANS
2	RAVENA	COEYMANS
3	COHOES	CITY
4	COHOES	CITY

If you want to extract separate data columns, the respective regular expression needs to be placed in different parentheses.

- **Uppercase:** Use the following command to change the area name to uppercase:

>>> df['AREA NAME'][0:5].str.upper()

0	RAVENA COEYMANS SELKIRK CENTRAL POLICE DISTRICT
1	RAVENA COEYMANS SELKIRK CENTRAL POLICE DISTRICT
2	RAVENA COEYMANS SELKIRK CENTRAL POLICE DISTRICT
3	COHOES CITY POLICE DISTRICT
4	COHOES CITY POLICE DISTRICT

Name: AREA NAME, dtype: object

And because the data strings are already in uppercase, not much difference will be seen anyway.

- **Lowercase:** Use the following code to in order to convert 'Area Name':

```
>>> df['AREA NAME'][0:5].str.lower()
```

0   ravena coeymans selkirk central police district

1   ravena coeymans selkirk central police district

2   ravena coeymans selkirk central police district

3   cohoes city police district

4   cohoes city police district

Name: AREA NAME, dtype: object

- **Filtering:** in order to filter rows on the OFFICER rank data, use the following command:

```
>>> df[df[' RANK LEVEL'] == ' OFFICER']
```

Chapter Four

Advanced Data Visualization

O ne of the essential tasks in data analysis or data science is making plots as well as interactive or static visualizations. Think of it as part of the exploratory process in which you can identify needed data transformations, outliers or even come up with model ideas.

Python has numerous visualization tools, but in this chapter, we'll delve deep into one known as Matplotlib. It's a multiplatform data visualization library that has been built around NumPy arrays and was made for working with the SciPy stack. The tool was developed by John Hunter in 2002 to enable the interactive style of MATLAB plotting interface in Python.

One of the best things about Matplotlib is how well it's able to play with various graphics back ends and operating systems. It supports a plethora of output types and back ends, which you can work with in spite of the operating system or output format required. Some of these formats include SVG, PDF, PNG, JPG, GIF, BMP, etc. It also has various add-on toolkits, including basemap for projections and mapping and mplot3d for 3D plots.

It is through the platform's everything-to-everyone tactic that makes Matplotlib very desirable in the hands of data scientists. Over time, the tool has garnered a huge user base, even leading to a highly active developer base, several powerful tools as well as ubiquity in the Python world.

You must have IPython started in Pylab mode (ipython --pylab) or have GUI event loop integration enabled using the %gui magic.

General Tips for Using Matplotlib

Before we get started on using Matplotlib for creating visualizations, there are some things about the package that you must know of.

How to Import Matplotlib

Similar to how we used to **pd** as a short-term for pandas and **np** for NumPy, we use basic shortcuts for imports from Matplotlib:

    In[1]: import matplotlib as mpl

        import matplotlib.pyplot as plt

Over this chapter, we will mostly be using the plt interface.

How to Set Styles

To pick the most appropriate style for the figures will be using the plt.style directive. We've used the classic style in the following to ensure any plot that has been created uses the standard Matplotlib style:

    In[2]: plt.style.use('classic')

We'll be adjusting the style all throughout the section when required.

Displaying Your Plots

If you can't see anything, there really is no point of visualization, but that depends on how much you're able to visualize your plots in Matplotlib. You can utilize Matplotlib the best way in the context that it is used: the three contexts in which Matplotlib is the best use is in an IPython terminal, and an IPython notebook, or a script.

Plotting from an IPython Terminal

Using Matplotlib within an IPython terminal interactively may be convenient. By specifying Matplotlib mode, IPython is made to work together with Matplotlib. You should use the %matplotlib magic command to enable it after you have started ipython:

In [1]: %matplotlib

Using matplotlib backend: TkAgg

In [2]: import matplotlib.pyplot as plt

From here, you can use any of the pyplot commands to open up a figure window, and several more commands can run with the plot that can be updated. However, a couple of changes (like when the properties of a line already drawn have been modified) will not be drawn automatically; you have to use plt.draw() to force the update. plt.show() isn't required in Matplotlib mode.

Using an IPython Notebook for Plotting

The IPython HTML Notebook is an online-based interactive computational document format or tool for data analysis that is able to combine the code, narrative, HTML elements, graphics, and so much more in one executable document. Since its introduction in 2011, it has developed into an excellent tool for interactive computing and the platform for reproducible teaching and research.

You can plot interactively with this notebook using the %matplotlib

command, and it works in the same way as the IPython terminal. With the notebook, you can even embed graphics into it directly using two of the given options:

- **%matplotlib inline:** leads to your plot's *static* images that have been embedded in the notebook.

- **%matplotlib notebook:** needs to *interactive* plots embedded within your notebook.

We generally utilize %matplotlib inline for this book:

In[3]: %matplotlib inline

Once the command is run and the plot created, any notebook cell can embed PNG images of the graphic:

In[4]: import numpy as np

x = np.linspace(0, 10, 100)

fig = plt.figure()

plt.plot(x, np.sin(x), '-')

plt.plot(x, np.cos(x), '--');

Using a Script for Plotting

If you're plotting from a script, you should use plt.show(). This function opens up an event loop, will look for any figure object that is currently active, and will open up either one or several interactive windows in which your figure/s will be displayed.

For example, if you've got a file titled myplot.py, it will contain this:

------- file: myplot.py ------

import matplotlib.pyplot as plt

import numpy as np

x = np.linspace(0, 10, 100)

plt.plot(x, np.sin(x))

```
plt.plot(x, np.cos(x))

plt.show()
```

Then you can use the command-line prompt to run the script, which opens up a window displaying your figure right in front of you:

```
$ python myplot.py
```

As this command interacts with your system's graphical backend, the operation's details will vary with each system and with each installation, which you can thank Matplotlib for hiding some of these details.

But one thing you need to take note of: the plt.show() command has to be used once only in every session and is usually seen at the script's very end. Several show() commands lead to uncertain back and-focused behavior and must be avoided at all costs.

How to Save Figures to File

A convenient Matplotlib feature is how figures can be saved in a number of formats. Saving a figure is done using the savefig() command so, to save our previous one as a PNG, you need to do is run this:

```
In[5]: fig.savefig('my_figure.png')
```

Now you've got a file titled my_figure.png in the working directory:

```
In[6]: !ls -lh my_figure.png

-rw-r--r-- 1 jakevdp staff 16K Aug 11 10:59 my_figure.png
```

To be certain that it has what it should have, the IPython Image object must be used to view the file contents:

n[7]: from IPython.display import Image

Image('my_figure.png')

Pythn infers the file format in savefig() using the given filename's extension. Many types of file formats, depending on the backends that have been installed, will be available. The following method of the figure canvas object will allow you to see the list of file types that are supported by your system:

In[8]: fig.canvas.get_supported_filetypes()

Out[8]: {'eps': 'Encapsulated Postscript',

'jpeg': 'Joint Photographic Experts Group',

'jpg': 'Joint Photographic Experts Group',

'pdf': 'Portable Document Format',

'pgf': 'PGF code for LaTeX',

'png': 'Portable Network Graphics',

'ps': 'Postscript',

'raw': 'Raw RGBA bitmap',

'rgba': 'Raw RGBA bitmap',

'svg': 'Scalable Vector Graphics',

'svgz': 'Scalable Vector Graphics',

'tif': 'Tagged Image File Format',

'tiff': 'Tagged Image File Format'}

When you save the figure, you don't have to use the plt.show() or any such commands that we talked about earlier.

Subplots and Figures

Matplotlib plots reside in a Figure object. You can use the plt.figure function to create a new figure:

In [13]: fig = plt.figure()

If you have pylab mode opened in IPython, it will open up a new empty window. plt.figure has numerous options, including figsize in which when saved to a disk, as a certain size and aspect ratio to it. Matplotlib figures even have a numbering scheme which replicates Matlab. Using plt.gcf(), a reference to the active figure can be given.

Of course, a plot can't be made with an empty figure. So to make one or more subplots, you need to use add_subplot:

In [14]: ax1 = fig.add_subplot(2, 2, 1)

This indicates that the figure has to be 2 x 2, so we start by picking the first four subplots.

In [15]: ax2 = fig.add_subplot(2, 2, 2)

In [16]: ax3 = fig.add_subplot(2, 2, 3)

When a plot command like plt.plot([1.5, 3.5, -2, 1.6]) is issued, the last subplot and figure used will be drawn by Matplotlib, hiding the subplot and figure creation. Use the following command will result in a figure after a single plot:

In [17]: from numpy.random import randn

In [18]: plt.plot(randn(50).cumsum(), 'k--')

121

The 'k--,' like the one using the command above, is a style option that instructs Matplotlib to draw a dashed black line. fig.add_subplot returns the objects that are known as AxesSubplot objects, allowing you to plug directly on any empty subplot by calling each of their instance methods.

In [19]: _ = ax1.hist(randn(100), bins=20, color='k', alpha=0.3)

In [20]: ax2.scatter(np.arange(30), np.arange(30) + 3 * randn(30))

Since it's a common task to use multiple subplots to create a figure per a certain layout, a new figure can be created using a convenience method known as plt.subplots and will have a NumPy array that contains the created subplot objects returned:

In [22]: fig, axes = plt.subplots(2, 3)

In [23]: axes

Out[23]:

array([[Axes(0.125,0.536364;0.227941x0.363636),

Axes(0.398529,0.536364;0.227941x0.363636),

Axes(0.672059,0.536364;0.227941x0.363636)],

[Axes(0.125,0.1;0.227941x0.363636),

Axes(0.398529,0.1;0.227941x0.363636),

Axes(0.672059,0.1;0.227941x0.363636)]], dtype=object)

This is quite useful given that the axes array can be indexed like a 2D array easily, such as axes[0, 1]. You also know that subplots have to have the same Y or X axis when sharex and sharey are used respectively.

How to Adjust Spacing around Subplots

There's a certain level of padding left by Matplotlib around the outside of subplots and the spacing between them by default. The spacing is specified relative to the plot's height and width, so if you were to use the GUI window to programmatically or manually resize the plot, the plot would adjust on its own dynamically. You can also use the subplots_adjust figure method to change the spacing easily:

subplots_adjust(left=None, bottom=None, right=None, top=None,

wspace=None, hspace=None)

hspace and wspace controls the percentages of the figure's height and width, respectively so that can be used as spacing between subplots. Here's what you can use to shrink the spacing right to zero:

fig, axes = plt.subplots(2, 2, sharex=True, sharey=True)

for i in range(2):

for j in range(2):

axes[i, j].hist(randn(500), bins=50, color='k', alpha=0.5)

plt.subplots_adjust(wspace=0, hspace=0)

Notice that when there is an overlapping of the axis labels, Matplotlib won't if check the labels have overlapped. So, in this case, you need to specify explicit tick locations and labels in order to fix the labels on your own.

Simple Line Plots

Visualizing one function, which is $y = f(x)$, is arguably the simplest out of every plot. Here will look at how you can create a simple type of plot. We start by having our notebook set up for plotting as well as porting the functions that will be using:

In[1]: %matplotlib inline

import matplotlib.pyplot as plt

plt.style.use('seaborn

Creating an axis and a figure is important for every plot in Matplotlib. Axes and a figure can be created in their simplest form when the following is used:

In[2]: fig = plt.figure()

ax = plt.axes()

In Matplotlib, think of the figure, which is a plt.figure class instance, as one container holding every object that represents graphics, axes, labels, and text. The axes, when it shows up, is a bounding box with labels and ticks that will hold the plot elements that go into the visualization later.

Once an axes is been created, try plotting some data using the ax.plot function. Let's begin with a sinusoid:

In[3]: fig = plt.figure()

ax = plt.axes()

x = np.linspace(0, 10, 1000)

ax.plot(x, np.sin(x));

Conversely, we can have the axes and the figure created for the background using the pylab interface:

In[4]: plt.plot(x, np.sin(x));

It is possible to use multiple lines to make one individual figure if we called the plot function several times:

In[5]: plt.plot(x, np.sin(x))

plt.plot(x, np.cos(x));

And that's all you need to know about simple Matplotlib plotting functions. We'll go into more detail about how you can control how the lines look in the axes.

Markers, Colors, and Line Styles

The main function of Matplotlib's plot will accept the arrays of X and Y coordinates as well as a string abbreviation optionally, which indicates line and color style. For instance, when plotting x against y using green dashes, you have to execute the following:

This matter of specifying both line style and color in a string is seen as a convenience; if you were programmatically creating plots, it could be that you prefer not to munge strings together to develop plots with the style of your choosing. You can also express the same plot more explicitly as follows:

ax.plot(x, y, linestyle='--', color='g')

Some of the regularly used colors have several abbreviations to them, but you can use any color by specifying its RGB value. There's a huge line of line styles when you look at the docstring for the plot.

In addition, line plots come with markers that highlight actual data points. Since Matplotlib creates a continuous line plot, it can be at times difficult to see where the points lie, when interpolating between points. The marker has to be part of the style string, which needs to have color along with line style and marker type:

In [28]: plt.plot(randn(30).cumsum(), 'ko--')

It can also be more explicitly written as:

plot(randn(30).cumsum(), color='k', linestyle='dashed', marker='o')

When it comes to line plots, you may see that by default, subsequence points are interpolated linearly. This can be changed using the option of drawstyle:

In [30]: data = randn(30).cumsum()

In [31]: plt.plot(data, 'k--', label='Default')

Out[31]: [<matplotlib.lines.Line2D at 0x461cdd0>]

In [32]: plt.plot(data, 'k-', drawstyle='steps-post', label='steps-post')

Out[32]: [<matplotlib.lines.Line2D at 0x461f350>]

In [33]: plt.legend(loc='best')

Adjusting the Plot

The first type of adjustment that you want to make is controlling the line styles and colors. The function plt.plot() takes on a variety of arguments that may specify these. For adjusting color, you should use the keyword color, which will accept any string argument that represents just about any color imaginable. We can specify the color in thse ways:

In[6]:

```
plt.plot(x, np.sin(x - 0), color='blue') # specify color by name

plt.plot(x, np.sin(x - 1), color='g') # short color code
(rgbcmyk)

plt.plot(x, np.sin(x - 2), color='0.75') # Grayscale between 0
and 1

plt.plot(x, np.sin(x - 3), color='#FFDD44') # Hex code
(RRGGBB from 00 to FF)

plt.plot(x, np.sin(x - 4), color=(1.0,0.2,0.3)) # RGB tuple,
values 0 and 1

plt.plot(x, np.sin(x - 5), color='chartreuse'); # all HTML color
names supported
```

If you don't specify a color, Matplotlib automatically cycles through a range of default colors for several lines.

Likewise, the lifestyle can be adjusted using the keyword linestyle:

```
In[7]: plt.plot(x, x + 0, linestyle='solid')

plt.plot(x, x + 1, linestyle='dashed')

plt.plot(x, x + 2, linestyle='dashdot')

plt.plot(x, x + 3, linestyle='dotted');

# For short, you can use the following codes:

plt.plot(x, x + 4, linestyle='-') # solid

plt.plot(x, x + 5, linestyle='--') # dashed
```

plt.plot(x, x + 6, linestyle='-.') # dashdot

plt.plot(x, x + 7, linestyle=':'); # dotted

If you want to be quick about it, you can combine the the following color and line style codes into one non-keyword argument to the plt.plot() function:

In[8]: plt.plot(x, x + 0, '-g') # solid green

plt.plot(x, x + 1, '--c') # dashed cyan

plt.plot(x, x + 2, '-.k') # dashdot black

plt.plot(x, x + 3, ':r'); # dotted red

These color codes of a single character represent the basic abbreviations in the CMYK (Cyan/Magenta/Yellow/Black) and RGB (red/green/blue) color systems, used mainly for graphics of digital color.

How to Customize Ticks

The default tick formatters and locators of Matplotlib have been designed as sufficient for most cases, but are not exactly optimal for all plots. We'll share examples of how you can adjust tick formatting and locations for a preferred plot type.

What we share the examples with you, you first have to know the object hierarchy of the plots in Matplotlib. There has to be a Python object in Matplotlib that represents anything the plot shows. For instance, remember that figure is the bounding box where plot elements show up. Every object in Matplotlib can contain sub-objects as well; for instance, every figure can have at least one axes object, in which each of those objects may have other objects that represent plot contents.

This is the same thing with tick marks. Every access consists of the x-axis and y-axis attributes, which they also post attributes that have every property of lines, labels, and ticks that go into the axes.

Minor and Major Ticks

With every access, you'll find the concepts surrounding a minor tick and the major tick mark. Like the names suggest, minor ticks are typically smaller, whereas the major ones are bigger and more pronounced. Matplotlib rarely uses minor ticks by default, and the only place they can be seen is inside the logarithmic plots:

    In[1]: %matplotlib inline

    import matplotlib.pyplot as plt

    plt.style.use('seaborn-whitegrid')

    import numpy as np

    In[2]: ax = plt.axes(xscale='log', yscale='log')

Here, we see that every minor tick reveals a smaller tick mark without a label, whereas in major tick displays a larger tick mark along with the label.

We can customize the properties of these ticks – namely labels and locations – by setting every axis's locator and formatter objects. Let's take a look at the plot's x-axis:

    In[3]: print(ax.xaxis.get_major_locator())

    print(ax.xaxis.get_minor_locator())

    <matplotlib.ticker.LogLocator object at 0x107530cc0>

    <matplotlib.ticker.LogLocator object at 0x107530198>

In[4]: print(ax.xaxis.get_major_formatter())

print(ax.xaxis.get_minor_formatter())

<matplotlib.ticker.LogFormatterMathtext object at 0x107512780>

<matplotlib.ticker.NullFormatter object at 0x10752dc18>

You'll notice how a LogLocator specifies every minor and major tick label locations. However, the labels of minor ticks are formatted with a NullFormatter, which means no label will be displayed.

How to Reduce or Increase the Number of Ticks

One of the usual problems that users encounter is that the smaller subplots can, at times, have crowded labels.

The numbers almost overlap whenever it concerns x ticks, which makes them really hard to figure out. Fortunately, you can use the plt.MaxNLocator() to fix this issue, as it specifies the total number of ticks that can be shown. With this high number, Matplotlib can choose specific tick locations by using its internal logic:

In[8]: # For every axis, set the x and y major locator

for axi in ax.flat:

axi.xaxis.set_major_locator(plt.MaxNLocator(3))

axi.yaxis.set_major_locator(plt.MaxNLocator(3))

fig

This makes everything appear much cleaner. And if you want even more control of the locations of those ticks that are regularly space, you can even useplt.MultipleLocator.

Adding Legends

Another crucial factor to determine plot elements are legends. There are a few ways in which you can add one, and the easiest way to do so is to have the label argument passed when plot function keyword has been added:

> In [0]: fig = plt.figure(); ax = fig.add_subplot(1, 1, 1)

> In [1]: ax.plot(randn(1000).cumsum(), 'k', label='one')

> Out[1]: [<matplotlib.lines.Line2D at 0x4720a90>]

> In [2]: ax.plot(randn(1000).cumsum(), 'k--', label='two')

> Out[2]: [<matplotlib.lines.Line2D at 0x4720f90>]

> In [3]: ax.plot(randn(1000).cumsum(), 'k.', label='three')

> Out[3]: [<matplotlib.lines.Line2D at 0x4723550>]

Once this is done, a lesson can be created automatically by calling either plt.legend() or ax.legend():

> In [44]: ax.legend(loc='best')

To let Matplotlib know where to place the plot, use the loc option. Or you can also go with 'best' if you can't decide on your own. To get rid of one or more of legend elements, don't pass a label or just do label='_nolegend_.'

Hiding Labels or Ticks

You can hide labels or ticks using either plt.NullFormatter() and plt.NullLocator() as shown below here:

> In[5]: ax = plt.axes()

```
ax.plot(np.random.rand(50))

ax.yaxis.set_major_locator(plt.NullLocator())

ax.xaxis.set_major_formatter(plt.NullFormatter())
```

Upon doing this, you'll notice how the labels have been removed from the x-axis, and how the ticks were removed from the y-axis. There are several benefits to not having ticks – like when you wish to show an image grid. Like when you want to show images of different faces which is typically used for problems related to supervised machine learning:

```
In[6]: fig, ax = plt.subplots(5, 5, figsize=(5, 5))

fig.subplots_adjust(hspace=0, wspace=0)

# Get some face data from scikit-learn

from sklearn.datasets import fetch_olivetti_faces

faces = fetch_olivetti_faces().images

for i in range(5):

for j in range(5):

ax[i, j].xaxis.set_major_locator(plt.NullLocator())

ax[i, j].yaxis.set_major_locator(plt.NullLocator())

ax[i, j].imshow(faces[10 * i + j], cmap="bone")
```

After doing this, notice how there is an axis to every image, and how the locators have been set to null at the tick values don't relay appropriate information for this type of visualization.

Drawing and Annotations on The Subplot

Besides basic plot types, you can also draw your own plot annotations, which can consist of arrows, text or any other shape.

Text and annotations can be added using the arrow, annotate, and text functions. Draw text at the given coordinates (x, y) using text on the plot along with optional custom styling:

```
ax.text(x, y, 'Hello world!',

family='monospace', fontsize=10)
```

Annotations are able to draw both arrows and text that are appropriately arranged. For example, let's take the closing index price from S&P 500 since 2007 and have it annotated with some of the dates from the 2008-2009 financial crisis. The result is as follows:

```
from datetime import datetime

fig = plt.figure()

ax = fig.add_subplot(1, 1, 1)

data = pd.read_csv('ch08/spx.csv', index_col=0,
parse_dates=True)

spx = data['SPX']

spx.plot(ax=ax, style='k-')

crisis_data = [

(datetime(2007, 10, 11), 'Peak of bull market'),

(datetime(2008, 3, 12), 'Bear Stearns Fails'),

(datetime(2008, 9, 15), 'Lehman Bankruptcy')
```

```
]

for date, label in crisis_data:

ax.annotate(label, xy=(date, spx.asof(date) + 50),

xytext=(date, spx.asof(date) + 200),

arrowprops=dict(facecolor='black'),

horizontalalignment='left', verticalalignment='top')

# Zoom in on 2007-2010

ax.set_xlim(['1/1/2007', '1/1/2011'])

ax.set_ylim([600, 1800])

ax.set_title('Important dates in 2008-2009 financial crisis')
```

More care should be given when it comes to drawing shapes. There are many objects within Matplotlib that represent a variety of common shapes, also known as patches. Some of the shapes like Circle and Rectangle can be found in matplotlib.pyplot, although you can find the full set from matplotlib.patches.

To give a plot its shape, a patch object known as shp must be created and added to a subplot by calling ax.add_patch(shp):

```
fig = plt.figure()

ax = fig.add_subplot(1, 1, 1)

rect = plt.Rectangle((0.2, 0.75), 0.4, 0.15, color='k', alpha=0.3)

circ = plt.Circle((0.7, 0.2), 0.15, color='b', alpha=0.3)
```

```
pgon = plt.Polygon([[0.15, 0.15], [0.35, 0.4], [0.2, 0.6]],

 color='g', alpha=0.5)

ax.add_patch(rect)

ax.add_patch(circ)

ax.add_patch(pgon)
```

Now, if you look at how most of the familiar plot types are implemented, you'll find it they have been assembled from patches.

Matplotlib Customization

Over here, will go through some of the runtime configuration options with Matplotlib and have a look at the stylesheets feature that contain a great set of default configurations, including color schemes that are geared specifically toward preparing figures for publications. Thankfully, most of its default behavior can be customized through a vast range of global parameters that control subplot spacing, figure size, font sizes, grid styles, colors, and more.

Changing Defaults: rcParams

You can interact with the Matplotlib configuration systems using two methods. The first method is rc, which comes programmatically from Python. Every time Matplotlib is loaded, a runtime configuration (RC) that contains the default style for each plot element created is defined. We can adjust this any time with the plt.rc convenience routine. Let's get a look at how the RC parameters can be modified just so the default plot is identical to what happened previously.

Let's save a copy of the ongoing rcParams dictionary, ensuring that changes can be reset in the current session:

```
In[1]: IPython_default = plt.rcParams.copy()
```

135

You can now change a couple of those settings with the plt.rc function:

```
In[2]: from matplotlib import cycler

colors = cycler('color',

['#EE6666', '#3388BB', '#9988DD',

'#EECC55', '#88BB44', '#FFBBBB'])

plt.rc('axes', facecolor='#E6E6E6', edgecolor='none',

axisbelow=True, grid=True, prop_cycle=colors)

plt.rc('grid', color='w', linestyle='solid')

plt.rc('xtick', direction='out', color='gray')

plt.rc('ytick', direction='out', color='gray')

plt.rc('patch', edgecolor='#E6E6E6')

plt.rc('lines', linewidth=2)
```

Now that you have defined these settings, a new plot can be created to see those settings at work:

```
In[3]: plt.hist(x);
```

Let's look at how basic line plots would look like using those parameters:

```
In[4]: for i in range(4):

plt.plot(np.random.rand(10))
```

This is much better than the default. But if you want to change it, you can do so by adjusting the rc parameters to what you want.

How to Customize Plot by Hand

For most of this chapter, we have learned how to tweak every plot setting to get something that is far more desirable than the default. Now we can learn how to customize these plots, starting with this dull-looking histogram:

```
In[1]: import matplotlib.pyplot as plt

plt.style.use('classic')

import numpy as np

%matplotlib inline
```

```
In[2]: x = np.random.randn(1000)

plt.hist(x);
```

We could take it further by customizing this histogram and will more aesthetically pleasing plot:

```
In[3]: # use a gray background

ax = plt.axes(axisbg='#E6E6E6')

ax.set_axisbelow(True)

# draw solid white grid lines

plt.grid(color='w', linestyle='solid')

# hide axis spines

for spine in ax.spines.values():
```

```
spine.set_visible(False)

# hide top and right ticks

ax.xaxis.tick_bottom()

ax.yaxis.tick_left()

# lighten ticks and labels

ax.tick_params(colors='gray', direction='out')

for tick in ax.get_xticklabels():

tick.set_color('gray')

for tick in ax.get_yticklabels():

tick.set_color('gray')

# control face and edge color of histogram

ax.hist(x, edgecolor='#E6E6E6', color='#EE6666');
```

Now the histogram looks visually appealing as it boasts the appearance of the visualization package of the R language's ggplot. This one requires a little bit more effort than some of the other plot-tweaking assignments that we've done so far.

Stylesheets

The following stylesheets are shown in plt.style.available, will start using the following five:

In[1]: plt.style.available[:5]

Out[1]: ['fivethirtyeight',

'seaborn-pastel',

'seaborn-whitegrid',

'ggplot',

'grayscale']

The standard way of switching to a stylesheet is calling:

plt.style.use('stylename')

It's important to note that using that changes the style for the remainder of the session. You can also use style context manager, which temporarily sets a style like:

with plt.style.context('stylename'):

make_a_plot()

Now let's develop a function that makes use of two basic plot types:

In[1]: def hist_and_lines():

np.random.seed(0)

fig, ax = plt.subplots(1, 2, figsize=(11, 4))

ax[0].hist(np.random.randn(1000))

for i in range(3):

ax[1].plot(np.random.rand(10))

ax[1].legend(['a', 'b', 'c'], loc='lower left')

We'll be using this to see how the plots look after using several styles built-in.

Default

For most of the book, we've only seen the default style. So we'll start off using that. The first thing you need to do is have the runtime configuration reset to notebook default:

In[2]: # reset rcParams

plt.rcParams.update(IPython_default);

Let's find out how it will look:

In[3]: hist_and_lines()

ggplot

In the R language, the ggplot package is extremely popular tool used for visualization. this style mimics that package's default styles:

In[13]: with plt.style.context('ggplot'):

hist_and_lines()

FiveThirtyEight Style

This style replicates the graphics there usually found on the FiveThirtyEight website. The results, as you will see, will be highlighted by thick lines, transparent axes and bold colors.

In[12]: with plt.style.context('fivethirtyeight'):

hist_and_lines()

Grayscale

Sometimes, you might prepare figures for a print publication that won't accept any color figures. That's why it would be better for you to use a grayscale style using the following:

In[1]: with plt.style.context

Dark Background

Sometimes, it's better to have a darker background then a light background, especially when it comes to figures that are used in a presentation. In order to get a dark background, you need to use this:

In[1]: with plt.style.context('dark_background'):

hist_and_lines()

Seaborn Style

Matplotlib consists of stylesheets that take their inspiration from the Seaborn library. When Seaborn gets imported to a notebook, these styles will be loaded automatically:

In[1]: import seaborn

hist_and_lines()

With all these options built-in for numerous plot styles, users find that using Matplotlib is quite convenient for interactive visualization as well as creating figures that will be published.

Chapter Five

Machine Learning

Before we look into details about several machine methods of machine learning, let's delve into what machine learning is all about.

The Definition of Machine Learning

Machine learning is a technique that teaches programs that make use of data on how to generate algorithms rather than having to program an algorithm explicitly from scratch. More specifically, machine learning involves having to build mathematical models that understand data better. The "learning" part comes in when the models have been given *tunable parameters* that can then be adjusted to observed data; this way, it would seem the program is "learning" from the data. When these models have been configured to previously known data, then they are able to foresee and understand the aspects of newly observed data.

It is important to understand that understanding of machine learning problems setting is crucial if users are able to use the tools more effectively. So let's start off machine learning with some of the broadly categorized stations of the kinds of approaches that we'll be discussing here.

Different Types of Machine Learning

Machine learning is categorized into three main types depending on the type of learning target or the feedback that's available to the learning system:

- **Supervised Learning:** this type of learning involves modeling the relationship between some label that is associated with data, and measured features of data; when this model has been identified, we can use it to apply labels to new types of data. That data is then further divided into regression and classification tasks: in regression, the labels are continuous quantities, whereas in the classification they are in discrete categories. We will look into examples of both of these supervised learning types as we go on.

- **Unsupervised Learning:** this is when the features of a data set our models without using any label as reference half and are usually regarded as "letting the data set speak for itself." There are several tasks in these models, like dimensionality reduction and clustering. Cluster algorithms are able to identify different data groups, whereas algorithms of dimensionality reduction look for data that are more succinctly represented. We will look into examples of two types of unsupervised learning later on.

- **Reinforcement Learning:** this is a program that dynamically interacts with the environment, like when it comes to driving a car.

Supervised Learning

Supervised learning algorithms will study the training data and then generate a function that can then be used to predict new instances.

Let's consider the example of a That training data is a bunch of text that highlights various news articles. The articles could be related to national, international, sports, business, and any other type of news category. Now let's take some of these categories as our labels. We will derive a couple of feature vectors using this training data wherein a certain word could be a vector, or several other vectors can be derived from this text. Let's say that the number of instances that the word "football" can be used as a vector, or the number of times the word "prime minister" can also be a vector.

These feature labels and vectors are then placed into the machine learning algorithm, which interprets the data. Once the model has been trained, will be used on the new data where the features will be extracted again and then fed to the model, and generate the target data.

Here's a couple of examples of supervised machine learning algorithms that will explain later:

1. Linear regression

2. Decision tree

3. The naive Bayes classifier

4. Logistic regression

Unsupervised Learning

As I said earlier, unsupervised learning refers to "letting the data speak for itself," which is another way of saying that it involves finding structures that are hidden in unlabeled data.

Let's take an example of some images that will act as our input and training data sets. The images contain faces of horses, insects, and human beings. Features are then extracted from these images, which are done to help the system locate the group that each of those images belongs to. The features are then fed it to the unsupervised machine learning algorithm that will, in turn, locate patterns within the data and then assist in bucketing those images to their respective groups.

This algorithm can even be used for new images and help to bucket those images into their respective buckets.

The following are examples of unsupervised machine learning algorithms that will be discussed in greater detail as we go on:

1. hierarchical clustering
2. The K-means clustering

Reinforcement Learning

When it comes to reinforcing learning, the data that will be fed to the machine learning model is offered as a stimulus from the environment to which the model has to respond and react. The feedback provided is like the teaching process, as we've seen with supervised learning, but rather as rewards and punishment in the environment.

The actions that the agent takes leads to it learning from the results that follow, instead of learning explicitly, and the action that it performs is based on its previous experience as well as the new choices that it makes, which in other words means trial and error. The agent gets the reinforcement signal, which takes the shape of a numerical award that will encode the success, and the agent learns to utilize appropriate actions that will boost the reward it accumulates over time.

Reinforcement learning is applied mainly in robotics instead of data science. Reinforcement learning uses the following algorithms:

1. Q learning

2. Temporal difference learning

Decision Trees

Decision trees are a simple model that is able to map an item's outcome to the input data. It's a well-known predictive modeling technique that is used all over the industry.

Decision tree models come in two types:

Classification trees: classification trees are basically a set of questions that have been designed to assign a classification. It can also refer to dependent variables that take a finite value. In these types of structures, the branches represent the rules of features that to class labels, and the leaves are the outcome's class labels.

Regression trees: this is when the dependent variable takes a continuous value.

Logistics Regression

Another supervised learning technique is logistic regression, which is essentially a probabilistic classification model. It's mostly used to predict a binary predictor, like when it comes to a fraudulent credit card transaction or when customers are looking to churn.

Logistic regression uses an equation as a means of representation, much like linear regression, which we will get to in a bit.

Using coefficient values or weights, the input values (X) are combined linearly to predict the output value (Y). It differs from linear regression because you can take any value from negative infinity to positive infinity and the output value is a binary value (0 or 1) instead of a numerical one.

Here is how a logistic regression equation looks like:

$$y = e^{\wedge}(b0 + b1*x) / (1 + e^{\wedge}(b0 + b1*x))$$

'y' the output that's been predicted, 'b1' is the coefficient for the single input value (x), and 'b0' is the intercept or bias term. Every column of the input data has an associated 'b' coefficient that should be learned from the training data.

If you're trying to plot a logistic function from a negative infinity to a positive one, then you have to use an S-shaped graph:

The following scenarios are where you can apply logistic regression:

1. The possibility of transformer failing using the sensor data that is linked with it.

2. Having a propensity score derived for a customer in a retail store buying the latest product that has been launched.

3. The chances of a user who clicks on an ad that was displayed on a website based on their behavior.

Linear Regression

Linear regression models are great starting points for regression tasks. These models are quite popular as they can fit quite easily and are quite interpretable. Maybe familiar with the most basic form of a linear regression model (like having a straight line fit into data). However, these models need to be extended in order to model data with more complicated behavior.

Over here, we will do a run-through of some of the mathematics behind this common problem, before we go ahead with how a model can be generalized to look into more complicated data patterns. Let's start with standard imports like the following:

In[1]: %matplotlib inline

import matplotlib.pyplot as plt

import seaborn as sns; sns.set()

import numpy as np

Simple Linear Regression

Let's start with the most familiar of linear regression, which is a straight line fit the data. This model comes in the form of $y = ax + b$, where 'a' is known as the slope, and 'b' is mostly known as the intercept.

Let's look into the data as follows, which comes with an intercept of -5 and the slope of 2:

```
In[2]: rng = np.random.RandomState(1)

x = 10 * rng.rand(50)

y = 2 * x - 5 + rng.randn(50)

plt.scatter(x, y);
```

Now let's use Scikit-Learn's LinearRegression estimator to have the state affect and construct the best-fit line:

```
In[3]: from sklearn.linear_model import LinearRegression

model = LinearRegression(fit_intercept=True)

model.fit(x[:, np.newaxis], y)

xfit = np.linspace(0, 10, 1000)

yfit = model.predict(xfit[:, np.newaxis])

plt.scatter(x, y)

plt.plot(xfit, yfit);
```

The data's intercept and slope are contained in the fit parameters of the model, which is usually indicated by a trailing underscore when it comes to Scikit-Learn. The relevant parameters for this are intercept_ and coef_:

```
In[4]: print("Model slope: ", model.coef_[0])

print("Model intercept:", model.intercept_)

Model slope: 2.02720881036

Model intercept: -4.99857708555
```

The results, as we can see, are quite close to the inputs.

However, the LinearRegression estimator is capable of much more than just this. Apart from straight-line fits, it also handles multidimensional linear models of the following form:

$$y = a0 + a1 \; x1 + a2 \; x2 + ...$$

Where there are several x values. Geometrically speaking, this is identical to a plane being fitted in three dimensions, or a hyperplane is being fit in higher dimensional points.

Regressions with such multidimensional nature are even more harder to visualize, but by using NumPy's matrix multiplication operator, we're able to see these fits in action by building some example data:

```
In[5]: rng = np.random.RandomState(1)

X = 10 * rng.rand(100, 3)

y = 0.5 + np.dot(X, [1.5, -2., 1.])

model.fit(X, y)
```

```
print(model.intercept_)

print(model.coef_)

0.5

[ 1.5 -2. 1. ]
```

The y data over here is built using three random x values, and the linear regression recovers the coefficients that were used to make the data.

This way, we can fit planes, hyperplanes, or lines to our data using the single LinearRegression estimator. And even though it seems as though this approach can only be used for linear relationships between variables, it turns out that this can be relaxed as well.

Naive Bayes Classification

Naive Bayes models are a set of simple, but extremely fast algorithms that are ideal for datasets of high dimensions. And due to them being fast and with only a couple of tunable parameters, they turn out to be quite useful and a quick baseline for classification issues. We'll focus on an intuitive explanation of the workings behind naive Bayes classifiers, along with examples of how they perform on several datasets.

Gaussian Naive Bayes

Gaussian Naive Bayes is possibly the simplest of the Naïve classifiers to understand. Here, the belief is that data in *each label is taken from a basic Gausian distribution*. Let's assume you have this type of data:

```
In[2]: from sklearn.datasets import make_blobs

X, y = make_blobs(100, 2, centers=2, random_state=2,
cluster_std=1.5)
```

plt.scatter(X[:, 0], X[:, 1], c=y, s=50, cmap='RdBu');

A really quick way to make a basic model is to think the data that a Gaussian distribution describes does not have any covariance between dimensions. We can fit the model if we find the point's standard and mean deviation within every label, all that is really needed for defining a distribution.

The Gaussian generative for every label will be represented in ellipses, with a larger chance towards the middle of the ellipses. In every class having this model, we have the simplest route to computing the likelihood P for any kind of data point, in which the posterior ratio can be quickly computed, and then we can determine which one of the labels is the most likely for a particular point.

This method has been utilized in Scikit-Learn's sklearn.naive_bayes.GaussianNB estimator:

In[3]: from sklearn.naive_bayes import GaussianNB

model = GaussianNB()

model.fit(X, y);

New data can be generated and the label predicted:

In[1]: rng = np.random.RandomState(0)

Xnew = [-6, -14] + [14, 18] * rng.rand(2000, 2)

ynew = model.predict(Xnew)

Now to plot the data so we can find the decision boundary:

In[2]: plt.scatter(X[:, 0], X[:, 1], c=y, s=50, cmap='RdBu')

lim = plt.axis()

```
plt.scatter(Xnew[:, 0], Xnew[:, 1], c=ynew, s=20,
cmap='RdBu', alpha=0.1)

plt.axis(lim);
```

In the results, we see that the classifications have a bit of a curved boundary to them – the boundary is quadratic.

One interesting part about this Bayesian formalism is it enables natural probabilistic classification, which is possible to compute when we use the predict_proba method:

```
In[3]: yprob = model.predict_proba(Xnew)

yprob[-8:].round(2)

Out[3]: array([[ 0.89, 0.11],

[ 1. , 0. ],

[ 1. , 0. ],

[ 1. , 0. ],

[ 1. , 0. ],

[ 1. , 0. ],

[ 0. , 1. ],

[ 0.15, 0.85]])
```

The columns show the posterior probabilities of the first two labels. If there is any doubt in the classification, then Bayesian tactics can be quite useful.

However, the last classification will be as good as the assumptions that result in it, and that is exactly why Gaussian naïve Bayes doesn't provide great results. Nevertheless, in most cases, this belief is enough to make Gaussian naïve Bayes obsolete.

Bayesian Classification

Naïve Bayes classifiers are built on methods of Bayesian classification. The methods are dependent on Bayes theorem, an equation that describes the relationship of conditional probabilities surrounding statistical quantities. For this type of classification, we find the probability of a label using observed features that are written as P(L | features). This tells us how this can be expressed in terms of quantities that we compute more directly:

$$P \ (L \mid features) = P \ (features \mid L) \ B \ (L) / \ P \ (features)$$

So for deciding among two labels (let's just call them L1 and L2) the only way to reach a decision is to have the ratio of posterior probabilities for every label computed as follows:

$$P \ (L1 \mid features) / P \ (L1 \mid features = P \ (features \mid L1) \ P \ (L1) / P \ (features \mid L2) \ P \ (L2)$$

What we need now is a model that we can get by computing P (features | L1) for every label. This model is regarded as a generative model as it specifies the hypothetical random process of generating data. Having this model specified for each label serves as the foundation for training when it comes to a Bayesian classifier. However, learning the fundamentals of this training can be quite difficult, but with the use of a couple of simplifying assumptions about the type of model, we can make the process even simpler.

And this is where "naïve Bayes" comes into play: if we were to make really naïve assumptions about every label's generative model, will be able to determine a rough approximation for every class's generative model, and then move ahead with the Bayesian classification. Every naïve assumption is dependent on a different type of naïve Bayes classifier. Let's start with the following standard imports:

In[1]: %matplotlib inline

import numpy as np

import matplotlib.pyplot as plt

import seaborn as sns; sns.set()

Multi-Nominal Naïve Bayes

Other than the Gaussian assumption, the multi-nominal naïve Bayes is another simple assumption that can specify every label's general distribution. It's here that we assume the features are generated via a simple multi-nominal distribution. This distribution talks about the chances of observing the counts among several categories, making it the most suitable for features representing counts or even count rates.

The concept is almost similar, except this time, rather than using the best-fit Gaussian for data distribution modeling; we will instead use a best-fit multi-nominal distribution.

Example: Classifying Text

Text classification is one area where we can use multi-nominal naïve Bayes, and that is where features give the relationship between word frequencies or accounts inside the documents set for classification. We'll use the word count features of the 20 newsgroups corpus to indicate how short documents can be classified into categories.

We can download some of the data and then look into target names

In[7]: from sklearn.datasets import fetch_20newsgroups

```
data = fetch_20newsgroups()

data.target_names
```

Out[7]: ['alt.atheism',

'comp.graphics',

'comp.os.ms-windows.misc',

'comp.sys.ibm.pc.hardware',

'comp.sys.mac.hardware',

'comp.windows.x',

'misc.forsale',

'rec.autos',

'rec.motorcycles',

'rec.sport.baseball',

'rec.sport.hockey',

'sci.crypt',

'sci.electronics',

'sci.med',

'sci.space',

'soc.religion.christian',

'talk.politics.guns',

'talk.politics.mideast',

'talk.politics.misc',

'talk.religion.misc']

We will choose only a couple of the categories for simplicity, and then download the testing and training sets:

In[8]:

```
categories = ['talk.religion.misc', 'soc.religion.christian', 'sci.space',

 'comp.graphics']

train = fetch_20newsgroups(subset='train', categories=categories)

test = fetch_20newsgroups(subset='test', categories=categories)
```

This is the data's representative entry:

```
In[1]: print(train.data[5])

From: dmcgee@uluhe.soest.hawaii.edu (Don McGee)

Subject: Federal Hearing

Originator: dmcgee@uluhe
```

Organization: School of Ocean and Earth Science and Technology

```
Distribution: usa

Lines: 10
```

If we want to use the data for the sake of machine learning, each string's content must be converted into a vector of numbers. That's why we're going to use the TF–IDF vectorizer for this and develop a pipeline that is attached to a multi-nominal naïve Bayes classifier:

In[2]: from sklearn.feature_extraction.text import TfidfVectorizer

from sklearn.naive_bayes import MultinomialNB

from sklearn.pipeline import make_pipeline

model = make_pipeline(TfidfVectorizer(), MultinomialNB())

Thanks to this pipeline, the model can be applied to the training data, and be useful in predicting the test data's labels:

In[3]: model.fit(train.data, train.target)

labels = model.predict(test.data)

When the test data's labels have been predicted, they can be evaluated to help us understand the estimator's performance. For instance, the confusion matrix between predicted and true test data labels are as follows:

In[4]:

from sklearn.metrics import confusion_matrix

mat = confusion_matrix(test.target, labels)

sns.heatmap(mat.T, square=True, annot=True, fmt='d', cbar=False,

```
        xticklabels=train.target_names,
        yticklabels=train.target_names)

    plt.xlabel('true label')

    plt.ylabel('predicted label');
```

But despite this simple classifier being able to differentiate computer talk from space talk successfully, it hits a snag when the discussion concerns religion, including Christianity. But this is to be expected.

Fortunately, we are now in possession of tools that can help us work out what category any string type is in, using the pipeline's predict () method. You can use the following utility function that will quickly return a single string's prediction:

```
In[5]: def predict_category(s, train=train, model=model):

    pred = model.predict([s])

    return train.target_names[pred[0]]
```

Let's give it a shot:

```
In[6]: predict_category('sending a payload to the ISS')

Out[6]: 'sci.space'

In[7]: predict_category('discussing islam vs atheism')

Out[7]: 'soc.religion.christian'

In[8]: predict_category('determining the screen resolution')

Out[8]: 'comp.graphics'
```

Just bear in mind this is a probability model for the frequency (weighted) of every word appearing in the string. Even still, the result is marvelous. In fact, when trained and applied carefully, even a very naive algorithm can yield surprisingly effective results on a large collection of high-dimensional data.

Hierarchical Clustering

Hierarchical clustering (otherwise known as also hierarchical cluster analysis) is an algorithm that collects a bunch of smaller objects and assembles them in groups known as clusters.

Data at several levels of a cluster tree or dendrogram are grouped together. It isn't just a single group of clusters, but rather a hierarchy of various levels where clusters at a certain level are grouped as clusters on the next level. Each of these clusters is distinct from other clusters, and the objects within these clusters are widely identical to one another. This will help you decide what level of clustering is ideal.

How Hierarchical Clustering Works

Hierarchical clustering begins when each observation is treated as a different cluster. After that, the following two steps are repeatedly executed:

1. Identify the two clusters are closest to one another
2 Merge those two clusters that are most identical.

This will continue to be the case until every cluster has been merged together.

There are two types of hierarchical clusters:

- **Divisive Hierarchical Clustering:** this is a top-down method in which a single cluster starts off observations that are eventually divided into two as they go down a hierarchy.

- **Agglomerate Hierarchical Clustering:** this is a bottom-up approach where every observation begins in its own cluster, which goes to two more clusters when going up the hierarchy.

K-Means Clustering

K-means clustering is one of the most popular as well as the simplest unsupervised machine learning algorithms around. It attempts to partition n observations into k clusters to ensure that every observation is associated with a cluster with the closest mean, that serves as the cluster's prototype. This eventually leads to data space partitioning into Voronoi cells.

This is so that the inner cluster data points are made as simple as possible while also ensuring the clusters are kept as far apart as possible. Data points are assigned to a cluster so that the sum of the squared distance between the cluster's centroid and the data points is at a minimum. The less variation there is in clusters, the more similar the data points will be within the same cluster.

How the K-Means Algorithm Works

In order to process learning data, data mining by the K-means algorithms begins with a group of randomly chosen centroid's that are used as starting points for each cluster, and then performs iterative (repetitive) calculations so that the positions of those centroids are optimized.

Creation and optimization of clusters see when either one of the two happens:

- The configured number of iterations has been achieved.

- The centroids have been stabilized – means the clustering has been successful, and there are no more changes in their value.

This method aims to solve the problem known as Expectation-Maximization. The E-step assigns data points to the cluster that's the closest. The end-step computes every cluster's centroid. Here is a formula of how it can be solved mathematically:

$$J = \sum_{i=1}^{m} \sum_{k=1}^{K} w_{ik} \|x^i - \mu_k\|^2 \tag{1}$$

Over here, wik=1 for data point xi if it belongs to cluster k; or else, wik = 0. Furthermore, μk is xi's cluster's centroid.

Example: K-Means for Color Compression

One very interesting way to use clustering is for compressing colors in pictures. For instance, let's say you've got a picture with over a million colors. For many pictures, a wide range of colors won't be used, and most of the pixels in those pictures will either have similar or maybe even identical colors.

Let's consider the example below from Scikit-Learn's

datasets module :

In[1]: # Note: the pillow package must be installed

from sklearn.datasets import load_sample_image

china = load_sample_image("china.jpg")

ax = plt.axes(xticks=[], yticks=[])

ax.imshow(china);

The picture is stored in a 3D array of size (width, height, RGB), where it consists of contributions of red-blue-green as integers from 0 to 225:

In[2]: china.shape

Out[2]: (427, 640, 3)

One of the ways to use this particular pixel group is as a cloud of points in a 3D color space. We can then have it reshaped to (n_samples x n_features], and then have the colors rescaled, so they rest between 0 and 1:

In[3]: data = china / 255.0 # use 0...1 scale

data = data.reshape(427 * 640, 3)

data.shape

Out[3]: (273280, 3)

Now using a subset containing 10,000 pixels, we can have these pixels visualized efficiently in the color space:

In[4]: def plot_pixels(data, title, colors=None, N=10000):

if colors is None:

colors = data

choose a random subset

rng = np.random.RandomState(0)

i = rng.permutation(data.shape[0])[:N]

colors = colors[i]

```
R, G, B = data[i].T

fig, ax = plt.subplots(1, 2, figsize=(16, 6))

ax[0].scatter(R, G, color=colors, marker='.')

ax[0].set(xlabel='Red', ylabel='Green', xlim=(0, 1), ylim=(0, 1))

ax[1].scatter(R, B, color=colors, marker='.')

ax[1].set(xlabel='Red', ylabel='Blue', xlim=(0, 1), ylim=(0, 1))

fig.suptitle(title, size=20);
```

In[22]: plot_pixels(data, title='Input color space: 16 million possible colors')

Gaussian Mixture Models

The K-means clustering model that we just explored was simple to understand. However, there were certain practical limitations as far as its application was concerned. Interestingly, the simplistic nature of K-means led to terrible performance for most real-life situations. Here, we are going to look at Gaussian mixture models, which may be considered part of K-means, but is also a robust estimation tool, more powerful than just simple clustering. We'll start with the:

In[1]: %matplotlib inline

import matplotlib.pyplot as plt

import seaborn as sns; sns.set()

import numpy as np

Shortcomings of K-Means

Now let's look at a few of the shortcomings of K-means clustering and how we can improve upon its model. We saw in the last section we covered that K-means clustering can find even more appropriate clustering results when data is simple and well separated.

Intuitively, one may expect that some points will have more certain clustering assignments than others; for instance, a small overlap between two center clusters exists in a way that we don't exactly have complete faith in the cluster assigning of points between them. Apparently, the K-means model doesn't have any intrinsic measure of uncertainty or probability of assigning clusters, which is why we have to generalize the model.

A way to look at this model is to see that it has a circle placed at the middle of every cluster, and the radius is defined by a furthest point in that cluster. This radius serves as a hard cut off for assigning clusters within the set meant for training: any point outside of the circle isn't included in the cluster. The following functions allows us to visualize those cluster model:

In[1]:

```
from sklearn.cluster import KMeans

from scipy.spatial.distance import cdist

def plot_kmeans(kmeans, X, n_clusters=4, rseed=0,
ax=None):

labels = kmeans.fit_predict(X)

# plot the input data

ax = ax or plt.gca()
```

```
ax.axis('equal')

ax.scatter(X[:, 0], X[:, 1], c=labels, s=40, cmap='viridis',
zorder=2)

# plot the representation of the k-means model

centers = kmeans.cluster_centers_

radii = [cdist(X[labels == i], [center]).max()

for i, center in enumerate(centers)]

for c, r in zip(centers, radii):

ax.add_patch(plt.Circle(c, r, fc='#CCCCCC', lw=3,
alpha=0.5, zorder=1))

In[1]: kmeans = KMeans(n_clusters=4, random_state=0)

plot_kmeans(kmeans, X)
```

One crucial Takeaway for the K-means model is that they have to be circular: there isn't a way built-in to account for elliptical or oblong clusters within the model. So if we were to use this data again and then transform it afterward, the cluster assignments would look confused and disoriented:

```
In[4]: rng = np.random.RandomState(13)

X_stretched = np.dot(X, rng.randn(2, 2))

kmeans = KMeans(n_clusters=4, random_state=0)

plot_kmeans(kmeans, X_stretched)
```

From the naked eye, we can see that the clusters that were transformed are noncircular, evidently indicating that these clusters were not a good fit. But, the K-means model is inflexible to the point where it can't consider this and will try to force the data to fit into four circular clusters. This leads to a mishmash of cluster assignments with the circles in the final product that will overlap: this is evident in the bottom-right of this plot.

The K-means model comes with two disadvantages:

    1. Lack of probabilistic cluster assignment

    2. Lack of flexibility in the cluster shape

Meaning it won't perform as we had hoped for many data sets.

One could think about generalizing the model to address the weaknesses; for instance, the uncertainty in the assignment could be measured through a comparison of the distances of every point to every cluster center, instead of focusing on one that is the nearest. You can also imagine making cluster boundaries as ellipsis instead of circles, just to take noncircular clusters. It turns out that these are actually two components of another clustering model type known as the Gaussian mixture model.

Chapter Six

Multiple Regression

Multiple regression is a statistical tool that enables you to examine how numerous independent variables are related to a dependent variable. Once you have determined these several variables and how they are related to a dependent variable, you can use every information regarding independent variables and then use it to make predictions that are more accurate and powerful about why they are as they are.

Let's take the example of a real estate agent who may want to record every listing the number of bedrooms, the size of the house (in square feet), a subjective rating of the house's appeal, and also what the average income in the respective neighborhood per the census data is. When information regarding several other houses have been compiled, it would certainly be interesting to know how and whether these measures are linked with the price concerning how a house is sold. For instance, you might find out that knowing how many bedrooms there are in a house to be a better indicator of the price for which a house is sold in a certain neighborhood than how "pretty" a house is to a certain individual, otherwise known as a subjective rating. You might also find out about "outliers," which are houses that could sell for more depending on their characteristics and location.

Personnel professionals basically use multiple regression methods to find out about equitable compensation. There is a number of factors or dimensions to consider, including the "number of people to supervise" (No_Super) or "amount of responsibility" (Resp) that might help contribute to a job's value. Then the salary survey among similar companies in the market is conducted by a personnel analyst, recording respective characteristics and salaries for varying positions. The information is then used in a multiple regression analyst says to construct a regression equation of the form like the one as follows:

$$Salary = 8*No\_Super + .5*Resp$$

Once this regression line is determined, a graph of actual salaries and expected salaries of job incumbents in a company can be constructed by the analyst. This is how an analyst is able to determine which position is overpaid (about the regression line) or underpaid (below the regression line), or paid equitably.

Another real-life situation is when natural and social science industries where multiple regression methods are commonly used in research. Multiple regression typically enables a researcher to ask (and perhaps also answer) the general question about "(what's the ideal predictor of...)." For instance, researchers of education wish to know what the best predictors of high school success are. Sociologists like to know which of several other social indicators can help best predict whether or not a new group of immigrants will get adjusted into society. Psychologists wish to know which personality variable is the best predictor of social adjustment.

Multiple regression estimates the β's in the equation:

$$y_j = \beta_0 + \beta_1 x_{1j} + \beta_2 x_{2j} + \cdots + \beta_p x_{pj} + \varepsilon_j$$

The X's in the equation are known as independent variables, whereas Y is the dependent variable. j is the subscript, which represents the observation number. The β's are known as the unknown regression coefficients and their estimates are represented by b's. Every β represents the original unknown (population) parameter, whereas b is an estimate of β. Lastly, εj is the error (residual) of observation j.

Even though you can use a variety of techniques to solve the regression problem, the most common method applied is least squares. In this form of regression analysis, the b's are chosen to reduce the sum of the squared residuals. This is the set of b's that you're looking for, given that they could be distorted by outliers – points that don't represent the data. Robust regression, which is opposite to least squares, aims to have the influence of outliers reduced.

Multiple regression analysis aims to study the relationship between the independent variables (regressors, IV's and predictors) and a dependent variable (response). The same equation for multiple regression would be:

$$\hat{y}_j = b_0 + b_1 x_{1j} + b_2 x_{2j} + \ldots + b_p x_{pj}$$

If $p = 1$, then the model would be known as a simple linear regression.

b0, which is the intercept, is where the regression plane would intersect the Y-axis. The slopes of the regression model are bi in the direction of xi. these coefficients are regarded as the partial-regression coefficients. Each of these coefficients represents the net effect the ith variable has on the dependent variable, making the other X's in the equation constant.

Much of the regression analysis focuses on analyzing sample residuals, ej, which are defined as

$$e_j = y_j - \hat{y}_j$$

As soon as the B's are estimated, several indices will be studied so that the reliability of these estimates can be determined. The correlation coefficient is one of the more popular liability indices to use. Also known as the correlation, the correlation coefficient is an index that ranges between -1 to 1. If he value gets close to zero, there will not be any linear relationship. When the correlation gets closer to either negative or positive one, the relationship becomes stronger. The value of either a plus or minus one means that there is a perfect linear relationship between two variables.

The regression equation is capable of measuring only straight-line or linear relationships. For example, if data forms a circle, regression analysis wouldn't be able to detect any relationship. Just for that, it's best to have each independent variable plotted with a dependent variable, watching for outline points, curves, changes in variability amount, as well as any other anomaly that may occur,

If the data you get is a random sample of a bigger population and that the εj are normally distributed and independent, a series of statistical tests could be applied to the correlation coefficient and the b's. The F-tests and t-tests can only be valid if the above conditions are met.

Regression Models

To properly use multiple regression, it is important that you have to have a fundamental understanding of the model. The formula for the basic regression model is:

$$y = \beta_0 + \beta_1 x_1 + \beta_2 x_2 + \cdots + \beta_p x_p + \varepsilon$$

The equation represents the relationship between the independent variables (IV's) and the dependent variable (DV) as a weighted average where the regression coefficients (β's) are taken as weights.

But unlike regular weights that are taken for a weighted average, regression coefficients can be negative.

In this model, it is basically assumed that every IV has an additive effect. Of course, no one actually believes the relationship is additive. Instead, they assume this model to be a commendable true model first-approximation. To get this approximation, further validity is an additive model that might even be considered to be the true model's Taylor-series expansion. Nevertheless, the appeal towards Taylor-series expansion typically gives the 'local-neighborhood' assumption a pass.

Another assumption is that the relationship between every IV and DV is linear (which is a straight-line). But once again, no one actually believes that the relationship is linear. Still, it would make sense for it to be a first approximation.

So to acquire better approximations, various models have been constructed to enable regression models to have curvilinear relationships approximated and also non-additivity. Even though nonlinear regression models can be applied in situations like these, they get the modeling process a higher level of complexity. An experience multiple regression user would certainly be able to tell where they have to include curvilinear components in regression models when required.

Another problem is how categorical variables can be added to the regression model. Categorical variables, unlike usual numeric variables, can be alphabetic. Categorical variables can be producer, location, and gender. To be able to use multiple regression models effectively, we have to know how categorical IVs can be included in these models.

In this section, we will see how NCSS can be utilized in specifying and estimating advanced regression models that include interaction, categorical, and curvilinearity variables.

Representing Categorical Variables

There are a few unique values that categorical variables can take on. For instance, let's C there are three possible values in a therapy variable: A, B, and C. Now, the question is, how do we get this variable into the regression model? One way we can do that is to have the letters converted into numbers by recoding the letter A to 1, B to 2 and C to 3.

However, if we were to recode A to 2, B to 3, and C to 1, we would be getting completely different results. This means that directly recoding letters to numbers is not going to work.

So to have a categorical variable converted to a form that we can use in regression analysis, a new group of numeric variables must be created. If, for instance, a categorical variable has K values, K -1 new variables have to be created.

There are several ways in which we can create these new variables. One way to do so is to use NCSS's Contrasts data tool to have new types of binary indicator variables and contrasts created automatically. Let's use a couple of examples right here:

Contrast Variables

Contrast variables are one of the popular types of generated variables in which several types of these variables can be created, some of which will be presented right here. One way to do so is to have each value contrasted with the reference value. The target value receives a one whereas the reference value gets a negative one, and all the other values get a zero.

What set of contrast variables are as follows:

T CA CB

    A 1 0

    A 1 0

    B 0 1

    B 0 1

    C -1 -1

    C -1 -1

The generated CA, CB, and IV's can be applied in the regression model.

Another group of contrast variables that are used recurrently to compare every value with the remaining ones. For this particular example, let's assume that T has over four values: A, B, C, and D. The generic variables are as follows:

T C1 C2 C3

    A -3 0 0

    A -3 0 0

    B 1 -2 0

    B 1 -2 0

    C 1 1 -1

    C 1 1 -1

D 1 1 1

D 1 1 1

Indicator Variables

Indicator (binary or dummy) variables are another set of popular generated variables. They are created when a reference value is first selected. For this type of value, the most common value must be chosen. After that, a variable for each value besides the reference value is generated. For instance, let's just say C is picked as the reference value. And for the rest of the values, and indicator variable is generated: A and B. The value of the original variable will be identical to the value of interest if the indicator value is one, or otherwise zero. The example below shows how to new indicator variables TA and TB and the original variable T look like:

T TA TB

A 1 0

A 1 0

B 0 1

B 0 1

C 0 0

C 0 0

The generated TA, TB, and IVs can be used in the regression model.

Representing a Curvilinear Relationship

A curvilinear relationship between one or more IVs and the DV is usually modeled when new IVs are added, the latter which is developed using the original IV by squaring and at times cubing them as well. For instance, the regression model as follows:

$$Y = \beta_0 + \beta_1 X_1 + \beta_2 X_2$$

Can be expanded to:

$$Y = \beta_0 + \beta_1 X_1 + \beta_2 X_2 + \beta_3 X_1^2 + \beta_4 X_2^2 + \beta_5 X_1 X_2$$
$$= \beta_0 + \beta_1 Z_1 + \beta_2 Z_2 + \beta_3 Z_3 + \beta_4 Z_4 + \beta_5 Z_5$$

Understand that in terms of the new IVs, this model is still additive.

Away for us to adapt to a new model is to have new IVs created using existing variable transformations. However, identical results can be acquired using the Custom Model statement. We'll explain the details about how a custom model can be presented later, but we will see that the model above can also be written as:

$$X_1 \quad X_2 \quad X_1 * X_1 \quad X_1 * X_2 \quad X_2 * X_2$$

Representing Interactions of Categorical and Numeric Variables

When the interaction between a categorical IV and a numeric IV is included in the model, everything proceeds as intended, except that an interaction variable for every categorical variable must be generated. Fortunately, this can be done in NCSS automatically with an appropriate Model statement.

The example as follows, an interaction between the numeric variable X and the categorical variable T is created.

T CA CB X XCA XCB

A 1 0 1.2 1.2 0

175

A 1 0 1.4 1.4 0

B 0 1 2.3 0   2.3

B 0 1 4.7 0   4.7

C -1 -1 3.5 -3.5 -3.5

C -1 -1 1.8 -1.8 -1.8

Representing Interactions of Numeric Variables

The interaction between two variables in the regression model can be represented when a new variable, which is the product of interacting variables, is created. For an interaction term to be necessary, let's say you have two variables including X1 and X2. You can generate a new variable by multiplying those two variables together:

X1 X2 Int

1 1 1

2 1 2

3 2 6

2 2 4

0 4 0

5 -2 -10

A new variable is then added to the regression model and will get the same treatment as any other variable during analysis. The interaction between X1 and X2 might be investigated with Int in the regression model.

Representing Interactions of Two or More Categorical Variables

When the model features interaction between two categorical variables, each combination of the generated variables for every categorical variable has to have an interaction variable generated. You can accomplish this automatically using an appropriate Model statement in NCSS.

The example below shows that the interaction between categorical variables S and T has been generated. Here, we will determine the reference value that was used for the variable S.

T CA CB S S1 S2 CAS1 CAS2 CBS1 CBS2

A 1 0 D 1 0 1 0 0 0

A 1 0 E 0 1 0 1 0 0

B 0 1 F 0 0 0 0 0 0

B 0 1 D 1 0 0 0 1 0

C -1 -1 E 0 1 0 -1 0 -1

C -1 -1 F 0 0 0 0 0 0

When variables, CBS1, CBS2, CAS1, and CAS2 are included in the regression model, they will be accounted for the interaction between S and T.

Assumptions

When using multiple regression analysis, the following assumptions should be considered:

Special Causes

We may assume that every special cause, outliers because of one-time situations, need to be removed from data. And if they don't, they could cause non-normality, non-constant variance, or any other regression model-related issues.

Constant Variance

For all values of the $X's$, the variance of the $\varepsilon's$ is constant. The residual plots of ej versus yj or the $X's$ can detect this. Should any of these residual plots display the shape of a rectangle, a constant variance can be assumed. However, if there is an increasing or decreasing bowtie or wedge-shaped from a residual plot, it would mean that in nonconstant variance is present and should be corrected.

Independence

It is assumed that the $\varepsilon's$ are uncorrelated with each other, which could also indicate that the Y's are uncorrelated as well. There are two ways in which this assumption could be violated: time-sequence data or model misspecification.

1. *Time-sequence data.* Whenever regression analysis is being performed on data that has been taken over time, the residuals are usually correlated. Correlation among residuals is known as autocorrelation or serial correlation. With positive autocorrelation, it could mean that the time period j 's residual is likely to have the same sign as a time period (j-k)'s residual, whereas k is the lag and time periods. Conversely, the negative correlation could mean that the time period j's residual could likely have the opposite effect in the time period (j-k)'s residual.

2. *Model misspecification.* If an incorrect functional form has been used or an important independent variable has been left out, the residuals won't be independent. The only way to fix

this is to include the proper independent variables or find a proper functional form.

Having autocorrelation present among residuals could lead to a number of negative consequences:

1. The mean square error could seriously be underestimated with positive serial correlation. The results that follow here are that standard errors have been underestimated, the confidence intervals are shorter than they're supposed to be, and the partial t-tests have been inflated.

2. Regression coefficients are unbiased but aren't efficient anymore, for example, minimum variance estimates.

3. Any confidence limits or hypothesis tests that require the use of F or t distribution would be invalid.

The serial correlation patterns can be identified informally, with residual plots against time. A better solution for this analytically would be to compute the autocorrelation or serial coefficient for varying time lags and then compare them to a critical value.

Normality
The ε's are believed to be normally distributed when confidence limits and hypothesis tests are used.

Multicollinearity
Multicollinearity, also known as co-linearity, refers to the presence of near-linear relationships amid a group of independent variables. All manner of problems with regression analysis is caused by the existence of multicollinearity, which is why it can best be assumed that data doesn't exhibit it.

Effects of Multicollinearity

Multicollinearity can inflate regression coefficients standard errors, create inaccurate regression coefficient estimates, give incorrect nonsignificant P-values, have partial T-tests for regression coefficients deflated, as well as hamper the model's predictability.

How to Identify the Triggers of Multicollinearity

If we are to solve the problems regarding co-linearity, we must be able to determine the source or trigger of those problems. The source is what affects the corrections, interpretation of linear models, and the analysis. There are over five sources to look out for:

1. *Physical constraints of population or linear model.* No matter the sampling technique used, this co-linearity source will exist. Most service or manufacturing processes have independent variable constraints, either politically, legally, or physically, which results in collinearity.

2. *Data collection.* Over here, data is collected from narrow subspaces of independent variables. Sampling methodology is what creates cold linearity. Acquiring more data on an increased range could remedy this co-linearity issue.

3. *Model specification or choice.* This collinearity trigger comes from user interactions from an original group of variables, or independent variables with higher powers. It should be considered that if the X_j sampling subspace is narrow, then any set of variables that include X_j will aggravate this issue even more.

4. *Over-defined model.* This source comes with greater variables than observations and must be avoided at all costs.

5. *Outliers.* Outliers, also regarded as extreme values in the X-space, cause co-linearity and can also conceal it.

How to Detect Co-Linearity

Here are the steps you can use to detect co-linearity:

1. First, study scatter plots of independent variable pairs in a pairwise manner, while looking out for almost perfect relationships. Also, for high correlations, take a look at the correlation matrix. Unfortunately, multicollinearity won't show up all the time, even when there are two variables at a time.

2. The next thing to do would be to factor the variance inflation factors (VIF). Larger VIFs indicate co-linear variables.

3. Lastly, you need to look into small eigenvalues of the independent variable's correlation matrix. An eigenvalue that is zero or near zero could indicate the existence of exactly in your dependence. But rather than using the eigenvalue's numerical size, you should use the condition number. Larger condition numbers mean co-linearity.

How to Correct Culinary

There is a multitude of solutions to consider depending on what causes culinary. If culinary was brought about by data collection, then we have to collect extra data over a wider X-subspace. If choosing a linear model has emphasized co-linearity, the model must be simplified by several techniques of variable selection. If culinary was induced by an observation or two, then these observations must be removed, and we have to proceed with caution. But more than anything, we have to use precision and care when it comes to choosing variables at the outset.

Scaling and Centering Issues in Collinearity

When regression variables are scale (by having their standard deviation divided) and centered (by having their mean subtracted), the resulting X'X matrix will be in correlation format. Each independent variable's centering has had the constant term from culinary diagnostics removed. Centering and scaling allow co-linearity diagnostics on standardized variables to be computed. Conversely, there are several other regression applications in which the intercept is essential to the linear model. The uncentered data's co-linearity diagnostics could offer a greater clarity of co-linearity structure in some of these cases.

Multiple Regression Checklist

The multiple regression checklist is a flowchart of steps, made by a professional statistician, that need to be completed in order to conduct a proper multiple regression analysis. The steps need to be completed in the proper order.

Step 1 - Preparing Data

You should have your data scanned for any the punch errors, anomalies, typos, and more. At least five observations for every variable in the analysis should be made, especially the dependent variable. We can assume that from this discussion that values go missing and random. Before using one of the variable selection strategies, every method of data preparation must be done.

Special focus should be given to categorical IVs to ensure that a relevant method of converting them to numeric values has been selected.

You also must decide how complex a model you should use. Should you include interactions between terms as well as variable powers?

One of the best methods to prepare data is to run it through the Data Screening method, as it offers reports about continuous and discrete variables, missing value patterns, and more.

Step 2 – Variable Selection

Variable selection reduces the amount of IVs to only a few that are manageable. Regression consists of a number of variable selection methods: Stepwise Regression, Subset Selection, Multivariate Variable Selection, or All Possible Regressions. Every one of these methods has its own set of pros and cons. That's why we suggest you start with the Subset Select method as it will enable you to look into powers, categorical variables, and interactions.

You must complete the first step before starting this one since outliers can greatly distort a variable selection. Finding outliers should be of the highest priority before starting the step.

Step 3 – Setup and Execute the Regression

Introduction

Now you can rest easy when it comes to operating the program. The NCSS was designed for simple operation, but it can appear to be complex at first. So the first thing you need to do for running it for the first time is to take a few minutes out of your time to read this chapter again and take into account the issues that come with it.

Enter Variables

The NCSS panels are already set for running by default, but it's important to select the proper variables first. You should have at least one independent variable and one dependent variable enumerated. Furthermore, if a weight variable from a prior analysis is available, it has to be specified.

Pick Report Options

There is a vast range of report options that come with multiple linear regression. As a starter, you'll mostly be interested in the regression equation's coefficients, serial correlation, variance report analysis, multicollinearity insights, and regression diagnostics.

Specify Alpha

Many statistics rookies forget about this essential procedure and allow the alpha value to default to the standard 0.05. You must make a more insightful decision about the kind of alpha value you want for your study. The 0.05 default surfaced during the time people were dependent on printed probability tables and that two values were available: 0.01 or 0.05. But now, the value can be set to whatever is relevant.

Choose Every Plot

It's rudimentary to choose every residual plot as everyone in them contributes a great deal to data analysis.

Step 4 – Inspect Model Adequacy

Introduction

As soon as the regression output has been displayed, you'll be prompted to go straight to the F-test probability from the variance table's regression analysis just to see if there are any significant results shown. However, you need to go through the output in an orderly manner. The most important conditions to look out for are related to normality, linearity, independence, multicollinearity, outliers, constant variance, and predictability.

Check 1. Normality

- Look into the Normal Assumptions Section. This section reveals a fit test's formal normal goodness. It's a decision for the normality (omnibus) test is accepted, then there's no way of knowing that residuals aren't normal.

- Look into the Normal Probability Plot. If any of the residuals come within the Normal Probability Plot, the normality assumption is probably met. At least one residual out of the confidence, bands could serve as a sign of outliers, not non-normality.

- If there isn't any normality, then take relevant action before returning to Step 2. Relevant action could be using the dependent variable logarithm or removing outliers.

Check 2. Linearity

- Look at the Residual vs. Predictor plots. If there's a curving pattern, it means there's nonlinearity.

- Look into the Residual vs. Predicted plot. If there's a curving pattern, it means there's nonlinearity.

- Observe the Y versus X plots. When it comes to simple linear regression, a linear relationship between X and Y scatterplots means that the assumption of linearity is appropriate. The same can be said if dependent variables are plotted against every independent variable in scatterplots

- If there is no presence of linearity, they take the necessary action and go back to Step 2. Necessary action could be to use a relevant nonlinear model or adding power terms such as X squared, X cubed, or Log (X)

Check 3. Serial or Independence Correlation

- If you have data regarding time series, the need to look into the Serial-Correlation Section, if there is a serial correlation in this section that's greater than the critical value that is given, then independence could be assumed.

- Look into the plot of Residual Versus Row; whatever the visualization that will be shown in this section will be indicated by adjacent residuals that are similar (a quick oscillation) or similar (a roller coaster trend).

- If there isn't any independence, then utilize a first difference model and go back to Step 2. More complex options demand time series models.

Check 4. Non-Constant Variance

- Look into the plot of Residual Versus Predicted. If there is a rectangular shape that is shown in this plot instead of a decreasing or increasing boat tire wedge, the variance will be constant.

- Look into the plots of Residual Versus Predictor. If there's a rectangular shape that is shown, instead of decreasing or increasing bowtie or wedge, then the variance will be constant.

- If there isn't a nonconstant variance, then take relevant action and go back to Step 2. Relevant action could be using weighted regression or taking the dependent variable's logarithm.

Chapter 5. Multicollinearity

- Look into the Multicollinearity Section. If you find any variable with a variance installation of more than 10, then co-linearity might be an issue.

- Look into the Eigenvalues of Center Correlation Section. Any condition number exceeding 1000 could indicate extreme co-linearity. Condition numbers that range between 100 and 1000 could indicate mild to strong co-linearity.

186

- Look into the Correlation Matrix Section. If there's any strong pairwise correlation found here, it could provide details about the variables that cause the co-linearity.

- If there is the existence of multicollinearity in this model, it might be because of strong interdependencies between independent variables or an outlier. If it's the former, then return to Step 2 and use another variable selection procedure.

Check 6. Outliers

- Look into the Regression Diagnostics Section. If you find any observation with an asterisk by the diagnostics Hat Diagonal, RStudent, the CovRatio, or DFFITS, that they'll be regarded as potential outliers. Any observation with a Cook's D that exceeds 1.00 can also be potentially influential.

- Look into the plot of Rstudent vs. Hat Diagonal. An observation being flagged in this plot could be influential by both diagnostics jointly.

- If there are outliers in this model, head to robust regression and run any of the options to confirm the existence of outliers. If the outliers are down-weighted or deleted, go back to Step 2.

Check 7. Predictability

- Look into the PRESS Section. If you find Press R2 to be almost as big as R2, then you will have done as expected. It's not uncommon for Press R2 to be half of R2. If R2 happens to be 0.50, then a 0.25 Press R2 wouldn't be acceptable.

- Look into the Predictive Values with Confidence Limits for Means and Individuals. If any confidence limit appears to be too wide for it to be practical, you might want to consider reassessing the co-linearity possibilities and outlier or adding new variables.

- Look into the Residual Report. Any observation with percent error grossly separate from most observation values serves as a sign that this observation could impact predictability.

- Define any changes in the model because of poor predictability, returned to Step 2.

Step 5 – Record Your Results

Because multiple regression can quite involving, it would be better if you take notes at various steps of your analysis. Be sure to note down whatever decision you make and what you have discovered. Explain everything that you've done, why you did it, the conclusions you have drawn, areas that need further investigations, which of the outliers you deleted, and more. Make sure to examine each of the given sections closely and in the order as it is shown:

1. Analysis of Variance Section. Inspect the model's overall significance.

2. Regression Equation and Coefficient Sections. Important individual variables are observed here.

Regression analysis is a complex statistical tool that requires frequent model revisions. Everything you've notified of the analysis process, along with the interpretation, will be worth it later on.

Computational Approach

In multiple regression analysis, the general computational problem has to be solved just so a straight line fit to several points.

In the simplest of cases – one independent variable and one dependent variable – this can be visualized in a scatterplot.

Least-Squares

In a scatterplot, there is an X or an independent variable, and a Y or dependent variable. For example, the variables could represent school achievement (such as GPA) and IQ (intelligence that will be measured by test), respectively every plot point represents a single student, which is the respective student's GPA and IQ. The aim of linear regression methods is so a line could fit through the points. The program will specifically have a line computed just so the observation points' squared deviations from that very line are reduced. Hence, this basic method is, at times, known as a least-squares estimation.

Unique Partial and Prediction Correlation

If you look at this equation closely, you'll see that the regression coefficients represent every independent variable's independent contribution to the dependent variable's protection. Another way this can be expressed is, for instance, the X1 variable is correlated with the variable of Y, once every other independent variable has been controlled. This correlation type is also known as a *partial correlation*.

The Regression Equation

A line in a two-variable or two-dimensional space is represented the equation Y=a+b*X; in complete text: the variable Y can be displayed in terms of a slope (b) and a constant (a) multiplied by the variable X. This constant can also be expressed as the *intercept*, while the slope can be expressed as the *B coefficient* or *regression coefficient*. For instance, GPA can be predicted as 1+.02*IQ. So, if the student has an IQ of 140, it would mean that their GPA would be 3.7.

R-Square and Residual Variance

The coefficient of determination, also known as *R-Square*, is a recurring statistic that is used to have the model fit evaluated. R-square is -1 the *ratio of residual variability*. Once the residual values' variability around the regression line to the variability overall is small, regression equation predictions will be good. For instance, if there aren't any relationships between Y and X variables, the Y variable's *ratio of the residual variability* will be 1.0 to the first variance. If that's the case, then R-square will be 0. If Y and X are related perfectly, then the ratio of the variance would be 0.0 and there won't be any residual variance, which makes R-square equal to 1.

Residual and Predictive Scores

The regression line portrays the dependent variable's (Y) best prediction, considering the independent variables (X). Nevertheless, the nature of this is hardly flawlessly predictable, and there is a substantial variation of observed points usually around the fitted regression line. The deviation of a regression line's particular point is known as the *residual* value.

How to Interpret the Correlation Coefficient R

Basically, the extent in which at least two predictors (X or independent variables) are related to the dependent variable (Y) is expressed in the correlation coefficient R, which is the square root of *R-square*. R, when it comes to multiple regression, can assume any value from 0 to 1. In order to interpret the direction of any variable's relationship, we have to look at the signs (minus or plus the current of the *B* or regression coefficients. If a *B* coefficient turns out to be positive, then this variable's relationship with the dependent variable would be positive as well; similarly, if the *B* coefficient were negative, then the relationship would also be negative. But then again, if the *B* coefficient were 0, then that would be any relationship between the variables.

Conclusion

In this book, we covered everything there is to know about NumPy, which is a library that offers the ndarray object for efficient manipulation and storage of dense data arrays and Python. Then we went over how you can manipulate data with pandas, which is a library that offers the DataFrame object for efficient manipulation and storage of columnar/labeled data in Python.

Next, we talked about a library known as Matplotlib in how it offers a range of flexible data visualization capabilities and Python. After that, We went over to discuss the various types of machine learning that are involved, including supervised and unsupervised learning, before finishing off with multiple regression.

All that's left now is for you to embark on a range of potential job opportunities that require sophisticated scientific computing tasks. Thank you and good luck.